THE
INLAND
ISLAND

A Year in Nature

Josephine W. Johnson

Illustrations by Mel Klapholz
Introduction by Camille T. Dungy

SCRIBNER

NEW YORK   LONDON   TORONTO   SYDNEY   NEW DELHI

Scribner
An Imprint of Simon & Schuster, Inc.
1230 Avenue of the Americas
New York, NY 10020

This Scribner trade paperback edition July 2022

SCRIBNER and design are registered trademarks of The Gale Group, Inc., used
under license by Simon & Schuster, Inc., the publisher of this work.

For information about special discounts for bulk purchases, please contact Simon &
Schuster Special Sales at 1-866-506-1949 or business@simonandschuster.com.

The Simon & Schuster Speakers Bureau can bring authors to your live event. For
more information or to book an event, contact the Simon & Schuster Speakers
Bureau at 1-866-248-3049 or visit our website at www.simonspeakers.com.

Interior design by Erika R. Genova

Manufactured in the United States of America

10 9 8 7 6 5 4 3 2 1

Library of Congress Cataloging-in-Publication Data is available.

ISBN 978-1-9821-7749-2
ISBN 978-1-9821-7750-8 (ebook)

THE
INLAND
ISLAND

THE PATH HER PEN DESCRIBES

I would have liked to take a walk alongside Josephine Johnson. To tromp, as she often did, across the thirty-seven Ohio acres she called home during the final decades of a life that spanned the twentieth century. To walk the land she let transform from mown pasture back to woods, and which she describes in *The Inland Island* with precise and clear-eyed care. I'm a walker, too, and I can feel in Johnson's lines the breath and tread of a person who measures time by the pace of her stride and the color of leaves on the limbs of trees. I would have liked to walk with Johnson, observing a huddle of ladybugs or the twisted trunk of an Osage orange, but she died in February 1990, at the age of seventy-nine, and I never had the chance. Reading *The Inland Island*, though, I feel as if she's right beside me, walking, walking, witnessing the world.

If I'd had a chance to take that walk with Johnson, I have a feeling she would not have talked much. She'd have been too busy watching and recording everything she saw. But I imagine she might have turned to me with the occasional question. "Do you want to go over and see what's growing near the clear stream, or the polluted one?" perhaps, or "What will you do today to protest the war?" or "Did you hear that robin singing from the wild cherry tree?" If *The Inland Island* is any indication, she wouldn't wait for an answer. Johnson writes in the present tense, as if she understands that what is required of us, always, is to be present, fully, in the place and time we are. As if she understood what had always been important and would remain ever so. She writes of the ugly and gorgeous in equal turns. This is a work of radical witness. Reading *The Inland Island* feels like being with Walter Benjamin's Angel of History, if the Angel of History were a midwestern amateur naturalist. Johnson does not judge, nor does she demand particular action from anyone or anything. She walks and she watches and she patiently describes.

The Inland Island was published in 1969, thirty-five years after Johnson's Pulitzer Prize–winning debut novel, *Now in November*. In 1935, at just twenty-five years old, Johnson became the youngest person ever to win the prize for fiction, and she remains the youngest person with that honor to this day. But *The Inland Island* is the work of a woman in her late middle age. This memoir, recording twelve months of her life on the land, is filled with the loving attention of someone who has learned how to live on through grave disappointment. The Vietnam War was much on her mind as she walked through the woods she'd let go back to the wild. Her son was facing jail time for activities related to antiwar protest, and she wonders about withholding her own tax dollars so as not to be party to violence she didn't condone. She thinks about Black people's struggles for equal rights. She wonders about what readers might think of her book, having faced dispiriting reception for some of the political stances she'd included in books she wrote after *Now in November*. She worries about the fox who roams nearby, a fox she knows local hunters want to kill. She considers what it must be like to be a caterpillar and, also, what it must be like to be a mink. She thinks about what it means to be American and white. "There are all manner of snow, both cruel and kind. There is the snow that falls like needles and drifts in hard ridges on the dead cornfields, is bitterly cold, coming down from the northwest and driving into the earth like knives," she observes, and I find myself nodding in chilled recognition. She writes about flowers and boorish neighbors with equal grace and precision and something that, even when what she witnesses hurts, I can best identify as love.

I would have liked to walk with Josephine Johnson across her thirty-seven acres. Thanks to this rerelease of *The Inland Island*, it seems as if I can.

Camille T. Dungy
Fort Collins, Colorado
December 2021

JANUARY

The new year lies before us. One stands on a high firm place. All's clean and clear. The air is fresh, not freezing. Hoarfrost is on the valley trees, grey ice on the pond and glitter on the grass clumps. The delicate dead grasses are frosted, the plowed earth cold and bitter-chocolate brown.

This beautiful slice of land is all that's left. It's my lifeblood. The old house is abandoned down in the valley where the mammoth bones were found in the quarry. We are on this side the ridge from that valley now. The children are gone. The horses gone. The old house gone. What's left? A world of trees, wild birds, wild weeds— a world of singular briary beauty that will last my life. The land— my *alderliefest*—the most beloved, that which has held the longest possession of the heart.

I was born of Franklins on my mother's side, and the Franklin was a landowner, a freeman, in the Anglo-Saxon days. I have had a love for the land all my life, and today when all life is a life against nature, against man's whole being, there is a sense of urgency, a need to record and cherish, and to share this love before it is too late. Time passes—mine and the land's.

This place, just short of the timber forty, has steep hills, two creeks, thousands of trees, and a network of small ravines or draws. There is one-half acre of flatland, and the house sits on it. The windows, wide as the walls, look out and down into a narrow valley made by a widening creek with steep clay banks. This creek bed grows in every storm, sometimes east, sometimes west. When it moves east it eats under the hill on which the house stands. In the storm nights one can hear the great rocks grinding in the rush of the water—rocks born in the beginning of the world, once the bottom of vast oceans—now upended, rolled and shoaled downstream, by a small midwestern storm.

The place begins at the top of the hill, a narrow entrance between old lilac bushes. There isn't any gate, only a space between the old barn and the lilac bush for cars to squeeze through, and every day one hears the crush and rattle of lilac twigs against glass. Which may annoy, and then may not—for no man or woman or child, coming down that drive for the first time, has failed to say, "My, but it's quiet back up here, I wish I had a place like this." I wish that they had, too. I wish there were great trees left and great trees planted. Who plants an acorn now for his son's oak? There's no room for oak trees in this world. And soon there'll be no room for sons.

The elm by the gateway is not like the beautiful wine-glass elms of New England, but it healed itself of a weeping ulcer, and it throws up a sturdy fountain of branches against the sky. Under it is the well, a well of deep cold water, whose pump was cured by the plumber of coughing up red clay. And the pump, the little rascal, as he gravely spoke of it in its gasping, seems his property, so closely has he come to be its master, its translator, friend and father. He knows its valves and snifters intimately, and only once did it catch him by surprise. The blacksnake in the rotor box. "You learn something new all the time," he said. "Everything has a first."

On the narrow ridge where the land begins is the old barn, the small willow-bordered pond, and beyond, a crumbling cottage where the original owners lived when this was once a farm. But uncultivated as it is now, steep and rank with dock and wormwood, I love it with a human-animal's love, and not a farmer's love. This place, with all its layers of life, from the eggs of snails to the eyes of buzzards, is my home, as surely as it is the wild bird's or the woodchuck's home. I'll defend it if I have to patrol it in the end with a bow and arrow—an old lady, like a big woodchuck in a brown coat, booting up and down these knife-cut hills, shouting at the dogs and hunters, making a path through the blackthorns and briars, a path through that encroaching ecology we were told would come inevitably as the tides, and faster.

This prophecy was from the state forester who tramped our thirty-seven acres, pointing out the wolf trees that spread up wild and branched, whose roots devour the wolf's nourishment and return only a few feet of trunk to man. No good for lumber, but home of raccoons and woodpeckers, riddled with worms and insects, source of life for the big eating-circle. "What can we do to make a nature preserve?" we asked him cautiously, the title belonging to vaster things such as the Serengeti Plain.

"Sit back," he said, "and watch the ecology develop."

That was all, and the tide of that odd word has come. With the sheep and horses gone, nothing tramps or grazes, and the blackberry vines' great red and purple hoops, their thorned whips, grow higher than a man's head. Nothing stops the elderberry shoots and the waves of goldenrod. The young trees follow the briars, and a forest begins in the pastureland.

The new year lies before us. Janus, the porter of heaven, opens the year. In Rome he was god and guardian of gates. His two faces were the gates that swing both ways. In times of war the gates of his great temple were always open. In peace they were closed. Only once between the reign of Numa and the reign of Augusta were these gates closed. In this year of our lives the gates are open. They have been open for a long, long time. The armies flow in and out. The war goes on.

In the mind's peculiar calendar, January is a high ridge, and the months go down, and now begins the slide toward spring. Winter is a time of clarity and simplicity. A time to begin, when there is less importuning, less distraction of the senses. The branches are bare and the far ridge visible. Through the bare branches the astonishing pileated woodpeckers flash and flatten against the scaly bark of the wild-cherry trees. From the back they look like huge cockroaches with red-crests. Black crows go laboring by, shouting, "Hawk, Hawk!" And under the angry convoy of their wings, a great grey hawk flies silently and lands on the white bones of a sycamore. He is blown up from cold to an owl's size, but the hawk head sits small and firm, the eyes ice-gold. There is gold on his wings and breast and he sits as though wrapped in the great feathered cloak of an Aztec king. White on his wings, white on his head, white in the great gripping talons. The cruel curved beak is empty. Cruel and curved? Have you seen the beak of a brown creeper? There's a scythe—a scimitar! Think how it looks to the small bark beetles. Hammered steel to them. A vicious thing and huge—the fishhook beak of this tiny bird like a speckled egg. His call is so thin and high it can't be heard at all except by the most acute of human ears. Around the winter trees he goes in a spiral. Invisible eggs and beetles delicately devoured as by a needle. His round and spotted belly is like the smooth pelt of the leopard seal, his outsize beak the narwhale's sword—that strange unicorn whale whose ivory tusk, superior to that of elephants, once made the thrones of Danish kings.

Our land is a paradise for woodpeckers. It is full of rotting stumps and trees and their scaling bark. The air is full of the black-and-white piano-key wings of woodpeckers and echoes with their constant drumming and banging, their harsh trilling, and the yak-yak of their frowsy clown, the yellow-bellied sapsucker. This solitary, selfish bird, who circles the trees with round regular holes, appears to have no mate. (Possibly, as Dr. E. Laurence Palmer says of the tapir, "they do not like each other.") His color is disturbing. A queer feeling comes in the stomach. This thick yellow-white, as paint squeezed from a tube, the blood-red double V on the throat like a slash, and the blackness of his wings. Now comes an image—a memory of carnival figures, the skeleton shape painted white on black, the red-and-yellow clowns in some Mardi Gras or Brazilian festival. There he is.

I am a bird watcher—a deeply interested observer. Not a bird lover. Their beaks are too sharp and their round eyes cold. I am fascinated by my fellow creatures of this planet home; but not fanatic, not scientific. We are too surrounded by specialists today to have pretensions of deep knowledge. Who can grasp the great migrations, or tell a wood warbler from a honey creeper by the absence of a fringed tongue deeply cleft, and the pattern of his jaw muscle? Can we see those important palatomaxillary bones always present except in adult *Icteria?* The great warbler master Ludlow Griscom has acid words for the amateur with pretensions. "Spring specialists, for whom the mastery of the fall migrations and the inclusion of the entire range of variation of the species calls for a memory completely outside their capacity," writes Ludlow

Griscom, "and they never try. I have known people thrilled at seeing a relatively uncommon species, unable to recall that they have seen it previously on several occasions. They were in the happy state of perpetually adding to their unkept life-list. This lack of factual memory seems to be the principal weakness of many women-birders."

My love goes out, perversely, only to the owls (as to warthogs, rhinoceros and walrus). I was brought up with domestic birds, and can still feel the puncturing beaks of nesting hens on my hands, and still have leg scars from wild young roosters, who regarded me, rightly, as their enemy.

But birds are beautiful and endlessly rewarding. There are more of them than the animals of this once, and future, forest, and a new bird makes the day. Down through the dry folded maple leaves that even in January cling like bits of orange paper comes a lone and lovely bird. Look! Where? There. Between the leaves. Can't see it. Look. Now over there! Where? There. Now it's moved. . . . Now I see it. There! Get the glasses . . . get the book. There's no time. . . . Just watch it. . . . Look. . . .

It's a bird with a moss-green body shading to brown as mossy stone, with wings painted sharply black and white. That's all. Any fool with eyes ought to find it in the book. But it isn't like anything in the book. It stays around. Days pass without our seeing it and then it appears again. It reminds me of the "snowbirds" that used to come in flocks after the first Missouri snowfall in my childhood. Briefly passing through as in a dream. But it isn't white. It is moss brown-green and all alone. We suppose at last it is the immature adult of some species which has migrated months ago, and this one, lost, lovely thing remains to baffle. (We find it is a goldfinch.)

We have our lists. We've kept them—"weak woman-birder"

though we be. (Quail, cardinal, white-throated sparrow, wren, dove, red-bellied woodpecker, junco, tomtit, chickadee, Lincoln sparrow, thrush, thrasher, bluebird, robin, red-tailed hawk, crow, barred owl, flocker and downy and hairy and pileated woodpecker. . . .) And then we read the annual January count, the professional-amateur count extending in a seven-mile radius all around us, and grow greyish-green with envy and astonishment. The ducks one has never seen, rare hawks, white owls, and sparrows with fringed tongues. And someone has always seen a gull. A gull inland? Aye, a gull. (I once saw a green parakeet, his long tail trailing in the mud of the barn lot. An astonishing sight—but not for the list. Somebody's pet. We wished him well but knew early death was for him.)

January in this core-land state, Ohio, oceanless, mountainless, tempered by rivers, is not a wild month of blizzards. Its range of weather is odd and unpredictable. There was the year of the rains when January brought not only snow, brought the rains, brought the flood, brought great desolate seas of mud. Came the sun and frost and thaw, storms of wind and hurricanes, ice, mud, slush, sun, frost, fog and rains. . . . The earth could not handle it. The hills, rigid with ice, by nightfall were sliding into the rivers. The creek roared yellow as the Yangtze waters of China. The ancient rocks laid down in the Devonian days were hurled downstream and shoaled like fish.

Creatures of habit could not survive the mad weather. Even the orderly, programmed birds learned to change. The juncos, who never fed off the ground before, came to the bird feeder and perched high in the trees, belligerent as the tomtits or chickadees. They dispersed their flocks as though knowing the ground might slide open and disappear with a roar under the weight of one delicate claw too many. For miles the flooded bottom lands were covered with ice-grey broken glass. The rivers so high and swollen they appeared to be silent and not moving at all.

But the usual year, the moderate year, begins bright and mild with some of the autumn's color left. Moss greens, green honeysuckle; here and there in the blackberry vines a rich red leaf whose stain of rust and crimson is an unexpected light, a glow like the cardinal in the winter dusk—the last eater, greedily devouring seeds in the twilight, almost incandescent in the cold gathering in the night. While all the other birds are about their business of preserving life in sleep, deep in the firs, or in the prickly nests of pasture cedars. On he munches.

And then, gradually, an increasing cold begins to drain this color from the trees and grass and ground, bleaching the unswept droves of oak and maple leaves. Sparrows peck at the grey ice. Moss turns grey. The ground, raked and reraked by the feet of quail, is dusty grey. The great hairy-beast coat of the pasture is bleached grey. No snow. No rain. Grey hawks in a grey sky under grey clouds. Grey cobwebs caught between the windowpanes.

The tree branches are stretched like grey nerves across the sky. The young opossum comes for the last time. He has not grown any larger, but that astonishing snowy fur is grey. He limps and holds one small-grey foot in a painful cramp. His great black mindless eyes seem clouded over. He would have done better to have gone to sleep when the woodchucks did, instead of wandering and getting wounded in the false-spring night. We saw him first in the early evenings of winter, tiny and perfect, a ball of snow-white fur the size of a guinea pig, each hair tipped in inky black, his eyes enormous and shining. He was completely unafraid, walking about duck-toed on the wet bricks, standing up on his hind legs, his nose held skyward, sniffing, his front paws like pink hands with squared-off fingers held on his chest. He tried to climb the pipe of the bird feeder, embracing the slick cold pipe with his little arms, hunching upward like an inchworm, only to slide backward and bump down. He gave up the effort after awhile and found a slice of toast on the ground, held it in those odd hands that appear to be pink roots sprouting from black gloves (the adventitious roots of corn or rushes that fringe the stalk above the ground). He bit with the nervous haste of rodents, and when finished waddled slowly toward the woods. The lopsided walk, toes pointing outward, this fur ball a comical and touching sight. It was sad to see him with the shadow over him.

As the winter cold deepens and tightens, the world, without snow, begins to turn from grey to white. The pond freezes over, is ice-white, milk glass. The willows turn white. Rocks ring. The sands of the creek bank separate. The gravel is dry and white. Everything's dry as though burned by sun. Grass white. Cattails white. The sycamore trees are great white bones. Everything's shrunk as far as it will shrink. Stones are smaller. Rocks shrivel. It tries to snow and the snow is only a silver dust in the air. One's lungs prickle. Cheeks get solid as tallow. Fingernails blue-white. It is a world burned white by cold.

In other years I spent good times in January brooding on some compensation for the winter, which seemed then a cold capricious tyrant, without virtues, without reason. If only it might bring some rich reward, something born of its own bitter coming. A choir of snow owls in the giant fir outside the window. A herd of wild, snow-whitened horses driven down from the north along the icy creek. And I thought, in large round childish language, of rich gifts. A stream of fruit from southern places. An overflowing, as when warm currents are driven into cold vacuums, and great ponderosa lemons would arrive, green avocadoes, oranges, grapefruit, mangoes . . . each on a grey day to appear in the grey sleet and the frozen grey mailbox. Packages still moist and warm, fern-sweet and fragrant from someone else's sun. A hot red sun, not the cold grey whale that swims across our sky in tents of canvas cloud. Or I would have settled for one walrus in the pond. Settled to see that great fat whiskered face with drooping tusks rise ponderously from the chilly water where nothing larger than a bullfrog ever rose before. Rise and descend, while the waters of the small pond overflowed the dam in a mighty wave down the hillside, freezing in terraces as it fell.

But now the extreme cold brings its true, appropriate gift—the narrowing down. Withdraw to one room. Put on your reading glasses. How astonishing the warp and woof of cloth. Marvelous the crystalline structure of a bottled honeycomb. Observe the sheer striated cliffs of broken gelatin for instance, the yellow ice floes, topaz fragmentation seldom seen before. Look into the bright red eyes of fruit flies born of ripening bananas. Behold the dust in the seams of the table, the rough gold pores on lemons, the cloudy patterns of cold coffee in the bottom of white cups. A revealed world here. And one's own hands. The whorls, striations, little mossy specks of brown, the strong thin bones like the sticks of a fan, the briar nicks, and the blue veins tunneling close to the surface. (The guessing game of childhood: "Which hand did I hold down?" "That one!" "How did you know?" "By the blood in the veins, of course, stupid!" Man, that was magic and science all rolled in one. And something one *did* oneself. That was the peak of it. Child, magician and scientist in the *now*. . . .)

The palms of one's hands are very different from the upper terrain. Turn the weathered and porous layer over. The palms are young still, and pink, the veins faint and small and the lifelines delicate, but ominous. "*. . . a long life—but you'll not be very well at the end*. . . ."

A long life ending in a long sickness. No. Not that for me. I've seen that. The tireless heart carrying the malignant flesh on and on through years of suffering. The family gathering and dispersing and gathering. The agonizing decisions left to the living, for one is not alive, one is not dead. Only the unspeakable limbo in between. The decisions of how much time and money and care and great science one must pour into the prolonging of this twilight torture are left to the living. Asking wisdom of the doctor who is not wise, asking answers of the surgeon who does not know, asking sisters and brothers, wives and husbands, *What shall we do?* And none dare give the answer that the sick flesh desires. *Let me die.*

Turn the palms over and hide them. Better the honest blue veins and knuckled bones. Examine the buds of cloves. There's something beautiful. Carved and precise with a prickling fragrance. One should age that way. Brown, dry, like spice.

The cold lasts a week, and then the heavy ice hand is lifted. The silent invisible wind that blew down the road like a river of ice ("I breathe Death every time I come down this road," the garbage collector said) has shifted. The morning sky is cloudy. It is like the inside of an enormous shell. Pale blue and pink, and the pond reflects its pearly light. Moderating influences have moved inward during the night. No hairy mammoths frozen upright in glaciers will ever be found in this middle land. Only the bones in gravel quarries.

In the winter sun I sat beside an old brother in the walnut grove. A rounded stone, boulder size, wedged hard in a narrow gully. Is it granite or sandstone or felsite or even limestone disguised by this rose-and-green surface, as though ancient lichen had been fired and fused into a milky glaze? I scratched around it with a stick to see its shape, which seems to be that of a roughly hewn potato. Not a great size, but too heavy for a man to lift. A sculptor would study it for the hidden form, cat, lion, bull . . . but I like this rock the way it is. The rough round shape is soothing. There's an orange scar on its side, and all around it lie the thin limestone rocks, swarming with sea creatures; rocks brittle, arrow-shaped or flat as grey flounders. But there's not a shell on this boulder, and it's sparkling with crystals, so we conclude it is granite, left when the glaciers melted; old, very old, and about the only thing of color now in the ugly hour of this particular bit of land.

For it *is* damn ugly, to be honest, here, right now. Rot, weeds, limbs fallen every which way, caught in young trees, crushing the shape out of them. Owl pellets under the sycamore. Scabby bark. Snow-brushed weeds flattened out into a shamble of sticks, burrs and briars. The walnut kills the vegetation beneath it, but the walnuts and the black snakeroot seem to have some mutually poisonous understanding. After thirty years, none of the trees are bigger around than a two-hand span, and hardly a nut among them. It's the hour for the stones.

They say now we are learning that the laws governing man and rock can scarcely be separated from each other. This small damp worm that humps itself across old brother, a measuring worm, black now and flecked with quartz, it moves and loops and moves, measuring for a grave, we said as children, and screamed and shook them off. What's he measuring here and in the heart of winter, laboring about intensely on my friend's great passive shape? Rock collectors are a pe-culiar people, I've been told. At night they put their rocks to bed. They count and cherish them as misers count gold. If I were mad, I'd sit and talk to this stone. There's much to be said of mutual interest. I would tell him of Stonehenge, by which the seasons were marked, the time of day, the coming of eclipses known. Henge means hanging, gallows-cross. Stone-brash is a land abounding in stones, stone-priest a lewd priest, and in the Falkland Islands are rock rivers, rivers of stone, chrystocrenes, whose origin is not fully understood by man.

And he knew the world of mammoths, and far back beyond. The nights of darkness when the great stones moved and mated. The monstrous grinding sound of love along the beaches, and in the desert moonlight huge forms rose and crashed; red sandstone kings went down in hurricanes of dust. Nights when the black rocks of old lava flows rolled in the surf—then rose, enormous as the whales, running with water from the tides, crashing, and then lay still. Huge, whole, and silent, for another century of time.

Down by the creek the banks are thawing as the month draws to its close. The calendar by which we live says it's the last day of January, this month of Janus, with four faces here.

The creek is not frozen. Down the steep brown banks, fine earth particles, separated by the freezing and thawing, trickle and flow into the creek. Fine and even as grains of sand. And whole rows of trees on the banks above, their hairy roots dangling in the wind, are doomed by these tiny trickles. Rocks that once lined the steep banks, row after row of sandstone snouts, old alligators sunning, are piled in the creek bed now. At the curve of the creek, in the layers of blue clay, red sandstone, grey slate, a thorn tree has held the bend for years, like some ancient grasping troll. Now only the tortured roots remain, the top broken off in a storm and tossed away.

The fine sifted earth slides down, and then a stone. A soft hissing sound, and then a splash. There's the land being carved and molded before one's eyes. There is the making of the world, in this sliding winter sand.

FEBRUARY

The crows are circling the house and shouting, establishing invisible territories. One lands. Opens and shuts his tail like a great dark fan. On the ground a covey of quail breaks in half with much in-fighting and musical quarreling. They are globes, bubbles, their feathers a rainbow of browns, and a lavender light on their tails. Feathers of every shape and size. Marvelous, the white streaks on their cheeks, the yellow glow around their eyes. They expand and contract like balloons, and the wind blows them.

The pink house finches drift through the woods. They look like English sparrows dipped in dye. Not a very good dye job, either. Then suddenly—*subito!* Above them in the maple tree is a bluebird. A patch of divine blue sky with a russet breast. It lifts the heart in an upward swing. There is no color like it in the world.

The grey squirrel, out on the end of a tiny twig at the top of the tree, gathers frantically. Stuffs some black, wet, leafy mass into his mouth, glides down the tree with this dark bale. Leaps up. Leaps down. Pauses to restuff his load with scratchy little fingers. Glides over a branch, glides under, arrives upside down on his black-cherry home. Rights himself. Disappears.

Three times he follows this invisible roadway through the trees, each time to gather this particular tangle at the perilous end of a branch. It may be bits of Virginia creeper. He is nest-building, and it is tiring to watch him jerking, running, jumping, snatching, and I am envious, sitting here, turning into a big soggy pear.

The owls are nesting. The great owls. They who "sleep by day and enter into the duties and pleasures of life by night." The Reverend G. S. Goodrich, of the *Illustrated Animal Kingdom* (1860), has a word for every situation in the world of nature. The owls, he feels, have been greatly misunderstood. A dread which dates back to Pliny, who described their calling as a "certain heavy groan of doleful mourning." "Their uncouth gestures," Goodrich says, "have led to mistaken attitudes. The owl is, in reality, a cheerful bird, singing, dancing, and rollicking in its daylight of darkness. A robin Goodfellow. In its moral qualities, it is most exemplary. Its parental devotion in prosperity and adversity is really worthy of admiration."

We have seen these great phantom shapes by day and heard them calling at high noon, which is a strange feeling. Disorients one. But stranger are the sounds at night. Once in the darkness by the pond a wild noise like a mule in pain brayed through the air, and another time from the ravines came weird slobbering sounds like nothing heard in life before. Uncouth indeed. The North American Indians, says Goodrich, call the owl *cobadecootch,* and the Cree speak of the snow owl as *wapohoo.* The French call the owl *chat-huant,* the hunting cat; and the Japanese, *howo-waiwo.* At times, they make pure, lovely sounds, and once, at night, listening to the conversation of owls—what owls I do not know, and will call the barred, as I know no better—they seemed to be practicing toot-toot in all its variations. Toot-toot, lovingly, gently . . . toot-toot loudly and firmly, toot-toot, like a ghostly tugboat in the stream of darkness. Toot-toot? A question. Do you love me still? Toot-toot! I do, I do. Back and forth, endlessly across the clearing, not hooting, not singing and dancing either, merely a monotonous loving conversation.

I picked up a little screech owl once long ago, dead in a patch of white violets, he was light as nothing; all those round shapes of owls are deceiving. Under the mass of feathers there are ghostly powerful bones, lightest aircraft in the world, temperatures up to 105 degrees (the little saw-whet who can file your nerves with his sound is hotter than the barred owl by one degree, and only the great horned owl burns harder). In the north pasture I found the freshly torn head of a mink, the blood still red, the beautiful black fur pulled backward from the skull and sharp white teeth. No sign of the body anywhere. Only this, left from that rush of knives in the winter night. A noble prey, as Goodrich would say, compared to the usual haul of mice and rats.

Winter is supposed to die this month. "The back of winter is broken," we say—a terrible expression, implying the old king still lives, moves, but is helpless and in pain. But the old king rises and scours the land with snow and ice, typhoons, blizzards, floods, sleet, deep snows from Texas to Maine. And one year, storms which hereto had raged around us in a vast circle—so that we, who had seemed to walk in a small dull island of grey weather, like a little grey man with an umbrella in the still heart of a cyclone—were suddenly swept with blizzards of snow and ice such as we had not known all winter.

And now a copious rain is falling. The creek is roaring and the cardinals singing. Yellow mud washes down from under the house. The daffodils are green shoot and green bud. Suet and pancakes are sodden on the bird feeder. The birds are sodden, too. The orange maple leaves, the pale tissue leaves from last fall, flap in the wind and rain. The cherry bark is washed black. Mats of grass are green. Two doves come. They have small pink feet and big wild eyes. They perch like two drops of grey dew on the branch.

The redbirds feed each other from the wet pancakes. Each twig has a delicate silver globe of rain, which clings even under the rain from the sky. The lichen is green and silver on the bark. Bobcats have been seen. A friend said she looked into their eyes.

Now comes the squirrel—sits on his southern balcony looking dry and gay, and shells a nut. My father always used to say of rainy days, "Good afternoon for a nap." The depressing and dreary sound of those words to us as children! Now I feel this ghastly post-prandial sleepiness creeping in like a fog. Dreary. Dreary! But safe—oh safe, as long as the rain is falling. Water rumbles down the pipes to the cistern. A big-headed hairy woodpecker comes. Looks like Punch. The hills are blue and lavender behind the trees. It is clearing. The feeling of safety recedes with the rain. The black trees shine.

The wind shifts to the north. The light of February begins.

There was a feast of purification held on the fifteenth of this month. Placed in the calendar by Numa, the second king of Rome. Maybe it was the light of February that brought it on. This white uncompromising steady light that shines through leafless trees. The days are long. The light is wide and high. No merciful shadow of leaves, no snow to cover all the trash of winter waste. It shines on everything. It stares—that unpleasant, long and level stare, the stolid and enormous eyes of children observing the antics of an adult world. This light shines on the shining beer can by the road, on each wad of wet tissue and thrown bottle broken in the grass. The heart of this month is its light. Cold, glassy, bright. All things revealed, beer can, burned peel, true goals, ugly souls, white bones, dead lambs, streams full of toilet bowls.

It shines upon ourselves, it is like a white glare in the mind. We know ourselves too well. We still need this February feast of purifying. It is always high noon, high court, in some desperate marble room of the mind. Overhead sun, overhead light. There we stand. Witnesses all around. Examined. Known.

I know myself in this terrible white light. One's a coward. One's timid and therefore treacherous. This is important to know. You can't be a little bit saintly any more than you can be a little bit pregnant. Sometimes the opossum faints with fear, sometimes he sinks those teeth in. The frantic mouse will bite. And all desperate animals will run, given the chance. Drive me out into this open field by the blows of conscience. Don't trust me. I'm timid. I'll betray you. I'll bite or run back in the damp dark draws. Out of sight, out of mind, I say. Bury your own bloody, bleeding dead.

It's the light doing this. The long steady stare of light.

It is terrible to be alone without a God.

He was a terrible God. I thought you liked to be alone.

There is someone, something, here. I am not alone. I am without protection.

What's there with you?

A black, smouldering thing.

Name it.

Integrity. Conscience. That which separates me from all these fortunate small animals, insects, birds and stones.

Wrap it up, stomp on it, drown it, bury it, frighten it, threaten it, run from it. . . .

I think it is disgusting
To praise God
For making us acknowledge His presence
By a poke in our eyeballs
With His sharp stick.

The state of my soul reminds me of a spring camel. My agnostic soul. Half-raw pink skin. Half-ragged rolls of decaying wool. The old shedding beliefs itch. The raw new skin exposed, lacking its old wool, is cold, cold.

I can't keep the horror of the burned children away. In April we will be presented with the bill for the burning of the children. And I can't separate the beauty of this place from the destruction of this place—the sewer water, the soapsuds, the hunters, the trappers, the dogs, the decay of the trees, the planes overhead, the sound of saws in the south, and the north and the east and the west. The target practice of the neighbors, the pollution of the air from sewers and burning garbage, from factories in the valley and even dust from Oklahoma. A world of war and waste.

Long before the feast of purification there was another festival. The Lupercalia, in which both dogs and goats were sacrificed, its rites conducted by the Luperci, the wolf-averters, they who traced a magic circle around the settlements to ward off wolves. After the sacrifice of animals, two priests were led to the altar, their foreheads touched with a bloody knife, and the blood wiped off with wool and milk. Then the ritual required that the two young men should laugh.

I pray you, my good Lord, lift this fog. Write about the merry. The merry mouse—or whatever can be thought merry in this winter world. All life is savage, so smile a savage smile at the pounce of the mouse on the bread by its hole. In and out like the snout of a seal from its hole in the ice. Bite, back up, reappear . . . and the tomtit sailing off with a potato chip like a sail in its beak and the soapsuds piling up in the creek. Entertain us owls with buck and wing. Sing owls, sing. . . . God, there must be something funny happening to tell. There are no clowns in nature. Man's a clown.

Laugh, young men of the Lupercalia, laugh.

IN THE WHITE LIGHT of February it is not well to stand here staring too long. Out-sights, not insights, we need now. What do I see clearly? The blue clay, the brown earth, the layers of sandstone rock. And from these banks a cold and pure spring runs. One of the few pure things left in the world.

And while I stand here in the white cold light, observing and observed, my husband passes, whistling cheerily, an enormous muddy bird, in his hand a trowel, on his back a muddy canvas full of fresh-dug clay. He toils up the steep hills, sliding on the wet leaves, the cold wet clay full of broken bits of stone, of bryozoan, and crinoid shells like salmon bones, weighting him down, a giant, upward-climbing troll.

In his mind is a vision. He is toiling up, cheered on by that vision. He is a potter, an amateur, a lover of that which he does. He sees some beautiful things, a pot, a bowl, begin to grow out of this earth, those bones and stones, old moss and ancient seas. The vision cheers him on. He does not examine his life in this searing light. He is intent on creating a life. He slips on the leaves, puffs and pants with his load, the deadweight of wet clay like a walrus on his back.

The vision cheers him down into the cellar, which is both damp and dusty, filled with tools, old newspapers, and the heaped detritus of five lives. There stands the great wheel he has made himself—two wheels, in fact. One's not perfect. Make another. He poured the great concrete wheel that turns the wheel head, built the wooden cage to hold the wheel. That old man in his wool and leather who invented wheel itself felt no greater triumph. Now he empties the big hunks of clay, plunks down his vision. Shells bite. Rocks bruise. The ancient Ordovician life resists him. The clay's not putty in his hands. He sets himself to master the clay. This is not easy. He lifts it up above his head and whacks it down. The thump and bang of earth goes on and on. If the earth's not welded, the pot's going to split and crumble. The hateful lessons of life begin to emerge in all their native starkness.

But at last his fingers feel they've got the stuff together, got the best of it, got the best out of it, and on to the throwing head it goes. Now the vision returns. Now's the time to think of life—out of that searing February light—forget what it's been, forget what it looks like without its leaves. Here's another chance. Here's this big homely clump of greasy grey clay, the old bones crunched up, shells fragmented, millions of years gone into the making, old wars forgotten, old feuds mastered, all the eating and being eaten, the winds gone over, the seas dried up. And here we are.

First you have to have a vision, you have to see what you want out of this unpromising bulk of old ancestral storms. It's there; it's been done—the miracle's no cheat. Then you have to get this lump exactly centered on the wheel; that's been done, that's possible, too. Man's a discriminating beast as well as a strong one—and then—oh, then—the turning and whirling begins. Get both hands around this clay, this life; around and around, and it starts to stretch and grow, and, as it stretches you have to know its "innate tensile strength," a master potter said—you have to know *this* clay's capacity to stretch, its exact point, beyond which, below which, it's not that which it could have been, the realization of its whole capacity.

(I have done those things which I ought not to have done, and I have left undone those things which I ought to have done, and there is no health in us. . . .)

The uncouth slippery lump athwart the wheel (or head) begins to rise, spiraling around and rising dizzily. The potter gouges down with thumbs inside, the hole begins to grow, the hollow heart enlarges. Hold on! The clay's still got some life of its own—it starts to weave and loop, lean outward, its eye on freedom—whole bowls have found escape, shot off the whirling head, found the farthest corner of the room, gone back to blob. My heart's been with them, but it's no use. Scoop yourself up—man's both master and clay of his own life. Dry off the wheel head. Plunk down, center the clay again. Grab the stuff with both hands and here we go again (in the end we'll thank those sharp thumbs in our eyes, won't we, O beautiful form, O wide and graceful flare, O vessel of the Lord). This is better than lying in the corner covered with dust cats, a mystery to night mice. Yes, this is a far, far better thing we be.

Grant has numbered all his bowls. The first is good for a beginner. Two is better. He tried bought clay, good, but not as hard, fiercely hard and red, as the clay from the creek banks. Some clay fires chalky white, feels chalky under the fingers. Looks unnatural, theatrical, as the white face of a *kabuki* dancer. (Not natural, eh? What's the land itself look like this morning? Miles of chalk-white snow all over the hills. Nothing's really *against* nature. Nature's got everything. A lot of which we don't like. The All-Mother was not made for man. The world is a place, not a home.)

Then there's the miracle of firing that turns this grey greasy clay into a rough, red brown that sparks with life. The miracle of glaze that shuts its pores. Makes rainbows. And the miracle of shape from shapeless clay. The potter's world is an extraordinary one. It's man's history and man himself. Grog, slip and slurry, flock, rib, and wedge, center and master. And in the end, burned earth, *keramos,* that which is rock and can never be softened or worked again. But can be broken.

IN THE MORNINGS OF hoarfrost, when the valley is a silver mist and the peach twigs rimmed with frost, there is the soft grey-blue of the jays, the magnificent stained-glass blue of the jay's wings and tail, balancing on the bending twigs. Or after a wet snow, each branch both black and white as a Japanese print, the sudden glowing luminous red of the cardinals, the rich and chestnut brown of the wrens.

A lone mateless mockingbird arrived in a miserable sleeting rain and set himself up a kingdom. He drove away the bluejays, the cardinals, the downy woodpeckers, even the great red-bellied woodpecker who could have tapped a hole through his head. The mockingbird sat in the middle of the peach tree above the feeder and decreed an invisible circle twenty feet around him, within which nothing larger than a junco was permitted. His range was determined in exact proportion to the size of the intruder. The downies and hairies came nearest to the invisible circle, the great redbelly he would drive the farthest. Six bluejays ganged up on him in one morning, but not one ever reached the feeder. He was the only bird I have ever seen who could fly backwards. And the only cries of the wounded were the screams of jays. He ate from his private table compulsively and, oddly, indifferently, as though to justify what was in truth not hunger but the lust for power.

Because he permitted the chickadees, the tomtits and the sparrows to feed within the invisible estate, he seemed to think of himself as a benevolent lord, establishing his lands to be held in fee for the weak, but it was more likely that there were simply too many of them to cope with, the meek and terrible power of numbers.

We wearied of his tyranny. We got tired of seeing nothing but small black and grey birds.

In the end we defeated him. By his own lust and our own kindness. We tempted him to enlarge his kingdom by establishing feeding stations all around the house; and for a while he fought valiantly to be everywhere at once. He flew from food pile to food pile in a dreary round of policing his now vast lands. He tried to see invisible poaching birds around corners, and then suddenly he grew tired. He settled for the back of an old wooden chair on the eastern side and slapped spitefully at the omnipresent chickadees. Once a day he made a token raid around the corner, but his old power was gone. The magic circle, maintained only by eternal vigilance, was broken; the big jeweled birds were back again, and instead of Tyrannosaurus Rex, the mocker was no more than a querulous old man waving his stick in the public gardens.

The crows continue an hourly, silent swooping back and forth near their old nesting place, as though clearing an invisible roadway for their building time. A snow-drop appears, green and immaculate with its white pendant flower. A mousehole appears in the snow right beside the flower. But it is not eaten. Doubtless the mouse comes out in the moonlight, gathers the corn fallen from the bird feeder, and plunges back into his hole with only a glance at the pale, pure drop that would taste no better than a cold pinch of dew.

Ghost cats belonging to someone else drift in and out. A huge black Persian, gone wild, lives around in barns and woods, but will not let any human come near. He is a monumental beast, like something-else disguised as a cat, the moth-eaten, matted Persian coat thrown hastily over the square bones of a beast built like a lion or a sawhorse. With two huge headlight eyes. Sometimes I see him padding past the house, making a strange pain-filled noise, but if he lifts his eyes to the window and sees me watching, he is gone. Even the dour opossums are friendly and clannish by comparison.

In the late afternoon the far hills are violet blue. In the sunlight the bare trees bloom like rose orchards, and under the peach tree an opossum sits eating a chicken bone. His wet pink nose twitches and twinkles as his tiny naked fingers hold the bone and his long ugly teeth tear off the meat. Then he turns and humps his way back along the edge of the wood, floundering in the snow, his long naked tail held out crookedly behind, his paws like human hands coming out from the black fur sleeves. He looks like a sick and hairy pig, to tell the truth. Once he was no bigger than a lima bean and even uglier than now.

But not uglier than his mate, the larger and hungrier female opossum who, bewildered by the untimely snows laid over the natural calendar of spring, curled up and went to sleep in the overturned garbage can. When found, she did not go into a faint but opened her jaws like a crocodile, stared with stately stupidity, and then moved away slowly toward the woods. She is *Didelphis virginiana,* largest and unloveliest of the possum tribe, in which are numbered the cuscus and the four-eyed possum and the tiny four-inch honeysucker, the golden woolly, and the mouse opossum who comes in forty-seven varieties and one hundred subspecies. But none of these are in North America, and we are left with *virginiana,* whom the Algonquins named opossum, meaning "white animal." And the Spanish spoke of her as "the remarkable Mother—the beast that hath a bag under her belly in which she carries her young, no bigger than raspberries, until they can shift for themselves." Her family goes back millions of years to the Mesozoic era, along with that common ancestor some claim we share—the minute and meddlesome minishrew. But the minishrew was *not,* like the oyster and opossum, content to let well enough alone; and instead, by devious pathways and millions of years, became the sources of both mammoth and man.

The "remarkable Mother" who emerged from the garbage can was no more a white animal than a grey kitchen mop whose hairy strands have all frozen separately up on end. And as she walked slowly away, testing the snow with her witch's hands, and looking back with her crocodile jaws agape, we thought of what strange things survived the abrasive years of time; unchanged, unimproved, and supremely ugly. A hairy old fossil, moved by the still-invisible tides of spring.

THERE ARE TWO SEASONS side by side on these steep hills divided by the creek. The northwestern hills that face the morning sun are brown with leaves and green with moss, the snow lies only in the hollow places. The southeastern hills are cold and white, the thin snow lies untouched.

In the pasture the snow-covered path has small footprints of some animal proceeding steadily alone. I do not know if it is a fox or dog. This snow writing is in a blurred and foreign script. And the edges of the tracks are rimmed and widened by an icy lace. Leaves of last year's mint and creeping moneywort are frosted with small watery crystals. We are certain of nothing except it is not the abominable snowman walking here. Nor is it the long-hunted, long-lost deer. More probably a tomcat.

Cross the creek and into early spring. The snow is almost gone, the leaves brown and wet, some even dry and blowing. A heavy growth of moss, a garden growing on a root, is fed by a melting bar of snow. Tiny petals of wild sedum like lily pads are buried in the moss, and in the sun it feels warm and spongy underneath your hand. How strange and beautiful this little tropic garden! Here on this hill is another granite rock, larger than my old friend in the walnut grove—twice as large, startling rich, and sumptuous with jagged bars of red rose quartz. It glitters and shines like an enormous jewel.

An owl has dropped a large grey pellet of ground bones on its head.

Push on up. A fallen giant tree so old and decayed I can't tell what it once was—but enormous—shelters a wild animal's hole. A very small hole outlined by doors or rock, well used. Large enough only for a skunk. And skunk it is. A faint unmistakable whiff as of sweet rubber burning, that wild gas unlike anything else in nature. Every now and then it comes, strong and then faint, as though one were stepping on old forms of yellow puffballs, those ancient domes that give off a perfunctory puff of spores and collapse. Knowing it is a wild thing's smell helps. No question about that. It's not a pretty fragrance.

There is a tall standing tree, stripped, skinned, polished of all its bark by the engraver beetles. Half their narrow homes lie in those long bark strips on the ground, the other half is written on the white and naked bole of the tree. Curious designs and hieroglyphs, Aztec sunburns radiating out from the beetle nest and then long straight corridors as hallways in a school, ending abruptly. The engraver beetle is an unusual insect, a patriarch who makes homes for all his wives. But the message is a death order. All through the woods are trees stripped down this way. Tall weathered bones.

But here's a small consolation now, a little cedar sticking up through the leaves. The size of a cocklebur. A Christmas tree for the lady-bugs. They're good beetles! A relief to think of them. Think of them, lying huddled by the thousands, cold red pools of red balls, beneath old logs and leaves, or huddled in the crevices of rocks, waiting for spring to warm them out so that they may go about their good works in the world. They may not be so thoughtful, so provident of homes for their wives as the engravers; they do not even have a wife or home; but they are one of man's few friends. So cherish the thought of them there under the snow. Round. Red. Cold. Good!

Up and over the second ridge, and winter's on the dark side of the hill again. The snow is full of tracks. It makes one feel blind and deaf not to know what's written plainly there. Tracks everywhere; every fallen log has been printed like a scroll. Feet have traveled across the creek, paused at holes, dived down holes, crossed other tracks. Mink, fox, weasel, possum, mice—all have left their messages, and I can't read. The tracks aren't like the tracks in books. Every beast has re-tracted his toenails. These little blurry blobs aren't like the precise five toes in the books. It's another language.

The silence behind the western ridge is awesome and complete. One's heart pounds from the beauty of it. The only sound is that deli-cate slipping sound of water moving under the ice, the movement of water like a snake rippling under the ice. The air bubbles flat, amoeba-shaped, some frozen, some free bubbles strung in rows like white beads. Crystal-cool and chalky. Three springs flow from the bank, pouring pure water from the thin blue rocks. They keep a wide, unfrozen pool which joins the stream and disappears beneath the ice.

Enclosed and magic world. Time stands still in the silence in the snow.

On the fallen logs, tracks run silently. A tree leans across the stream and is lodged far up in the branches of a beech. It is rimmed with snow and the tracks run up, small creatures running up to heaven. Or to eat, or to die. Mink may play here in the darkness.

From a wounded beech there hangs a great icicle of frozen sap. There is the sweet smell of wet leaves, wet earth, or sun on snow and moss.

In the stream is another granite boulder. This is the greatest of them all—great for our part of the world at the far edge of the glacier's coming. It is a worn ancestral boulder of grey-pink granite, smooth, no jagged crystals, white with snow, green with old lichen. Enormous. I sit beside the stream, a brown humped boulder, and we contemplate in the silence, in the snow. The cool slipping of the stream between us, the world beyond the hills does not exist. Only this white ravine, these prints of wild feet in the snow.

The feeling of all this unknown creature-life that passes and re-passes here brings on a curious dream-like feeling of enchantment. It is the seed of fairy tales, the seeking of lost valleys. Timeless pockets in the world of time. Either I should not ever leave, or I should not return again.

MARCH

The hear-hear of the cardinals in the cold is an icy sound. Knuckles on glass. It will sound different in April. The great wicker cage of the forsythia bush, which covers thirty feet now, is turning yellow. It has moved outward from a moderate bush to this wild tangle—as the banyan tree expands—up and then down, to root in an ever-widening circle of curved earth-seeking arches and wild, unrooted shoots. A beautiful mess, a witch's hair. An open cage, through which the birds pour all day long, or sit in sullen lumps to feel the morning sun. Rabbits and opossum move along its floor; it is the quails' way station in their endless circling of the land—a line of bright, speckled globes, brown heads, they run into this wild witch shelter. The hawk beats silently away. The voices of the quail are strange and sweet. A cat pounced on one female in the flock and she carried a grey ragged patch directly in the center of her back where all the neat, exquisite feathers had been torn away. She was not crippled, but the purplish skin was bare for a long time, circled with grey down.

The hill edge is rimmed with daffodil shoots, falsely called forth, betrayed by snow and ice. Yellow-sheathed buds surviving grimly. This is a new month because a little bunch of squares on the calendar says so. Once it was the year's beginning. The Saxons called it *Hlydmonath,* loud and stormy month. Around and around the seasons go, and every year the gaping mouth of March, the windy month that breaks the season open. Mars, god of war, lengthening month, and out of this month flow lengthening days, wind, leaves, and war, torn crows and promises. O promises.

There are brick-red elm buds against the sky. The far hills appear lavender instead of grey. Or do I imagine this because I turned the calendar page over? Month of the bloodstone, that strange stone of polished plasma, green with red spots, those drops that represent the blood of Christ in our mythology of gems.

How long can I go on pretending the world is not changed beyond recognition? The blood from that one nation which we ravage flows all over the world. It flows into my mind night and day. Blood, despair and rage. It's not frozen into a stone. It's living blood and it's turning black, not red.

The traditional March winds have been around for several months, but now they come again, leaf lifting, tree shaking. It is terrifying to see a huge tree move and shake clear to its roots. Or does it only *seem* to move? The branches whip and bend, they strain, and the roar of the wind strikes terror to our hearts and we think the tree has moved from bud to root. The wind is glorious and pagan. It blows the dust of our lives a thousand miles. We read the dust. If there's a deadly message in it, that's for us to know. The wind comes bearing things with it, lifting up, sweeping on. The great invisible river that has no need or knowledge of us.

No, I don't like to walk in the wind and the rain. The rain gets on my glasses and down my neck. It chills me and there's no fire inside. The wind's an enemy, too. Except the joy of hiding from it, finding a hollow haven in the leeward side of a ravine. It seldom turns corners. Like the ancient Chinese ghosts, it must flow straight ahead. Weak, furry creatures watch from holes. Birds flatten against the bark. The crow locks his knees. One doesn't find the small perching birds in heaps like tumbleweeds, so they survive somehow. Shoulder up in the heart of the prickly cedar. Cover their eyes with their wings or hole down in their feathers, flatten their crests. The leaves, not mashed by ice and heavy snow, break up, turn on end. Dry leaves start awkwardly on brief journeys, wild risings, brown and ghostly dispersions to a traveling nowhere and a huddling under the thorns.

Rain turning to snow.

Terrible headache probably caught from sick buzzard at the zoo.

The quail come through the snow, which is steady and slanted, not aimless; thoughtful, as in slower snows. The quail rouse up the leaves, make disorderly beds. The snow covers them. The grass sticks up green hairs, The daffodils stick up, their pale heads watery and discouraged. The delicate cold petals of forsythia open in the house. A triumph. A success. It makes one feel among the great gardeners at last. Didn't rot; didn't slump; didn't wait until its brethren outside were also in full bloom. These frosty fingers I regard with awe again.

The near trees are stark black. The far trees a net of white webs, the far hills grey. Now the snow shifts its pattern. The steady slant turns to a spiral. The flakes seem larger, rounder. Some trees are turning green with lichen. Yesterday the fields were alive with flocking robins. When the robin flies down he does not flutter, he drops. When he eats, he pulls at his food, as though pulling a worm out of the ground. He lifts the leaves in his beak and tosses them aside. He jerks up the crusts of bread.

The forsythia cage has turned pure white. An arched net of snow. The delicate grey juncos line its inner branches. Its buds are white. It has caught and caged every flake of snow that's fallen. And under the snow run the thin gold lines of sap. The forsythia came from China and is related to the olive. *Forsythia suspensa* has hollow upright branches, *Forsythia intermedia* has arched branches, and most forsythia are hybrids of *F. intermedia,* which was the offshoot of *F. viridissima* and *F. suspensa,* the wild olive ancestors from Asia. *Intermedia* is a dull name for these great arching bridges and branches, half in heaven, half in earth. It's *viridissima—virere,* to be green, *vire,* the arrow-feathered, to achieve a rotary motion . . . *vir,* to turn . . . virent, freshness . . . to shoot up . . . up and turn . . . burrow down and rise again . . . *virbiasses* . . . being twice a man (and *sississimus* is Swahili for red ants—are you with us still?).

This is *suspensa-viridissima* that we have here, not just a squatty *intermedia,* studded with barn sparrows, huge brown buds on every hoop.

The snow is slowing down. A trilling comes. Some early amorous bird. The cardinals feed each other. A courting gesture. He offers her a sunflower seed. Her beak is full already. He jabs away. Eventually his loving peck is received. Usually it's better handled, better beaked, a sweet reciprocity.

He stretches lean in his courting song. His crest stretched up, his whole body thinned out as he sings, watching the female, tung tung tung . . . the strained persistence of a single note. She flies away. He flies down to eat, Light, but not heat.

The ground is whiter, whiter, the bark greener. The mournful sound of the Norfolk and Western hoots up the valley. It rolls up two miles through the snow.

The quail are eating and down comes a squirrel, snow-frosted pink-rimmed eyes, icy little claws. What is the quail attitude toward the squirrel? They stop eating, they huddle together, and each and every quail turns its back toward the squirrel and stares off into the distance. He rummages about, digs up snow-covered bread, runs away. They turn around and resume their eating. A curious sight. How does he feel? He doesn't give a damn. He is long gone with his greasy bread.

It appears to be snowing birds—sparrows and juncos, tomtits and chickadees, woodpeckers and cardinals, and suddenly a robin is snowed down.

May God make the snow fall on this terrible war. Bury the armor. Cool the burned.

THE YEAR MOVES ON toward spring. The wicker cage of the forsythia grows more yellow every day. They used to call these changeable days "the dangerous weather." Every day is dangerous now, climatewise and otherwise. For three months there have been these shiftings, these extremes.

Woke one morning to an extraordinary snow. Deep soft blanket world. Great white elephants looming everywhere. The honeysuckle and the fence a hairy mammoth. The wind released the pine branches slowly—a long exploding tip of pine moves in a circle, like the sensitive tip of an elephant's trunk.

On the green-grey ice of the pond a caravan of camels is kneeling. Strange shapes everywhere. The garbage cans like giant popovers. Two men with guns. "We didn't see no signs." One was kneeling in the road, his gun pointed at the field's "No Hunting" sign.

A world too beautiful, too strange for words. After awhile the sun and wind turned all the snow into something mad and messy. Suds, batter, dashed against the trees. The snow on the ground was pitted from odd falling clumps off the branches. Once a load descended like a falling bird with outstretched wings that shattered into light.

Showers of snow fell in a veil before the sun. All through the woods white birds flying and falling. And yet it was silent. Lovely and silent and blazing white.

Then, in a few days, the warming began. The invisible melting.

Spongy ground. The dry hummocks of grass squashing under foot into the snow ooze. Saw tadpoles in the brown water of the pond and, dimly, mossy encrusted crawfish crawling near the shore. The algae rose in green clumps with curious rootlike hangings, green Medusas. The ground is pitted with mouse and mole and shrew holes. It looks like a big brown cheese around the bird feeder. Bees are out; mosquitoes. Big black ants appear on the sink.

That kingfisher sound was a flicker. I should have remembered that peculiar call. It paused briefly, high in black cherry. (Was it a flicker the opossum gnawed, at the Beckers, sitting preposterously calm on the flood-lighted lawn, his little nasty hands shuffling yellow feathers, spreading the wings like a fan before his face, and gnawing the bloody bones?)

Two doves flew down. Indescribable softness of their color, pink over grey; the shape of doves is maddeningly beautiful. Their feet were pink in the moss. They have tiny little heads. Their descent, awkward, nervous, twittering, is a disaster more than a descent. Their rising is labored and noisy. They are so slow only their extreme nervousness saves them. But beautiful—oh, beautiful—dove grey, dove rose, dove blue, and the exquisite lines of their stupid little heads. They drive the bluejays away.

Very warm in the woods. The big creek filthy—a greasy grey like an enormous flowing of dirty dishwater with tiny particles as from thousands of human teeth pickings. Hardly wanted to get my boots wet in it.

But the second creek is pure and flowing over the stones. Sweet wet earth smell. Sat by the large granite boulder, almost green now, orange where the water edged around it. Found two silvery nests of vireos still knitted well with the moss between. No birds. No tracks. Only the leaves on the move. Leaping up, tugging at the thin frozen blanket of themselves, moving about like squirrels. Got scared by a rabbit bolting out from his shelter. Sounded louder than a gunshot.

Stroked a fallen log covered with moss as though it were a green, living thing. A cloud of yellow pollen blew from my hand. Other logs had every crack filled with the oyster-shaped fungus of *Stereum versicolor,* some small and greyish, upright as oysters, shoved in the cracks, and the larger spread as the tails of drumming pheasants, beautiful with copper bands, brown, grey and mossy-green bands, damp and velvety smooth to touch. Another fungus grew with them, less distinctly banded, whose underside was ridged and folded, *Daedalea quercina,* which means worked cunningly, and labyrinthine—after Daedalus who made the Minotuar's deep winding labyrinth. A heavy name for this crimped and greyish bit of stuff! I would like to find a *Polyporus squamosus,* which they say grows seven feet in circumference, forty-two pounds in weight, and all this colorful expansion in four weeks alone. Found, instead, a root so resembling the head of a goat that horns, ears and beard were clearly there, a rude yet delicate resemblance that startled.

It grows almost hot in the ravine. The air is soft and damp, a soft light breeze at times. The creek is running well. The cold water flowed through hollow cow bones on the pebbles, the air full of little white things flying. And on a rock a lively coal-black springtail brisked about. The bright-green varnished shoots of star-of-Bethlehem came up in clumps, and the pure-white bulbs were exposed along the creek where the earth had washed away. Moss everywhere—green moss on stones, on logs, bright emerald green. The tree across the creek that slants up skyward is covered with moss now, snow all gone. The only whiteness, odd, bleached rocks stranded here and there, returning to their old shell color. And there are flat square stones, grey, ominous, chiseled with laws, like some mosaic tablet (or one could think of them as stone sandwiches instead, very old and stale).

Someone has upturned a big stone under a tree, its earth side raw and exposed. And has ripped a great vine from the tree and knocked it aside.

The stream is crossed and recrossed by fallen logs. And on one a mourning-cloak butterfly sits in the sun, slowly folding and opening his dark wings edged with cream. A red so dark it is black. A phoebe has come, but it is silent. The only sounds are the crows and the creek.

Almost invisible under the leaves, the salt-and-pepper flowers are opening with a faint honey scent. And from a fresh hole comes a puff of skunk. The scarlet cup fungus are open. Bright cardinal mouths among the leaves.

And then comes a more believable March day. Harsh, cold. The week of warmth and sun has urged everything forward in preparation for this grey descent, this icy air, this icy mist. Fold on fold, over every bud, every gold daffodil. Every premature arrival. Get them up. Freeze them out. Chill. Chill. It's some ghastly gothic joke that's played each year.

The forsythia fountain looks alive though, runs yellow in all the hoops, and all the hoops are hung with yellow drops, the unopened flowers arrested by the cold. Above them the elms are a mass of brown buds, brown lace. The redbirds are shrill, deceptively cheerful.

It's a good cold day for burning. Three thousand scraps of paper bearing things of importunity and word of man's sinning, cries for help, and stuff for sale. The very things you save accumulate until they press you down. Too much of everything. I am obsessed with the thought of starting over. Starting again with everything gone. A March thought. Fifty-seven years of accumulation. But man is not earth. He does not change to marble under pressure. Just assumes a curious shape. Living conglomerate.

> "Conglomerates represent consolidated gravel, and always indicate an aqueous origin, often the delta of an ancient stream or the invasion of sea over land. Important to geologists in interpreting past events."

WELL, HERE WE STAND. A mass of rounded pebbles of varying sizes cemented together. A few of boulder size, but all rounded in water and transported a great distance. Waiting to be interpreted. Blue clay, yellow clay, and some geodes, hollow and lined, surprisingly, with beautiful crystals. These lumps gathered around some hard and undissolving memory. Love, failure, hate—or that lost ice-cream soda on the streetcar ride. The refused, the ungiven, the undone. These lie inside like fossil insects, but in some no nucleus can be found. No leaf. No shell. No bone.

The brown buds are cold and so is the mist. The spongy earth is cold. The green moss is icy. The frogs have sunk back in the mud again. (Did you ever feel that the cold feet of frogs were walking over you?

No. Only hot insects biting at random all night long.) Birds should be migrating this way soon. Something to add to our unkept life-list.

Now is the time for taking stock. What do we have to deal with here? Shut the door. Or put your shoulders against the wind. Stomp on stuff coming up. Hold it down. We've got to have a quiet moment here. Tides of life and tides of decay, and all more silent than the sea.

What can we learn from the past? What teach? Our experience is vinegar. Mother-of-vinegar. *Mother,* this strange transparent stuff. Membrane of yeast cells and bacteria, added to wine and cider to start vinegar (and also—for the record—mother is *modder,* is mud). How can I live in two worlds? As you have been living. Torn, divided, growing by shreds and wounds, growing by ridicule. Until one resembles the astonishing corn plant emerging from rolled and shredded newspaper. Behold the poet, the ragged and upright soul of man.

The poets were honored men in the old days in Ireland. They had a place then. Voices of wisdom, bearers of tidings, good, bad, true, invented, newsmen and singers. We're a small bunch today. Fellow tapirs. We cannot understand each other. Gather seven hundred together in a kingdom? One hundred in a castle? I wouldn't spend the night there. But things were different then.

I had a strange thought this month in the wind and snow. A vision of the Coming—not the Second Coming, that dream of Christians, but a Coming of a man from the Arctic, marching slowly down. Brown, broad, majestic. Great, flat, moon-shaped face. Black eyes. A pagan man to deliver us from our bloody and binding dreams. To deliver us from our stinking wars of religion, wars of patriotism. Our wars in which we use the bodies of burned children to ward off our childish nightmares of a Communist world. Our war for democracy in which we blind, burn, starve, and cripple children so that they may vote at twenty-one.

THE BUD ENDS OF box-elder twigs look like hard green roses. Green stem, green rose, tough buds. Smooth and wiry branches. Very tough. Formed like the horsetails, the ancient plants. Scarred already, and only a year alive. There is a chill wind, and the clouds are edgeless and thin.

APRIL

In two days the great forsythia cage, a vast mound of green wickets hung sparsely with yellow bells of flowers, the first leaves fine as a mist, has become a wild monster. Hairy, green, bushy, green-toothed and horned.

The birds no longer perch forming delicate Japanese paintings of the old school. They disappear. Who knows what goes on inside, now.

A great hare, dark and slow, huge as a domestic rabbit gone wild, lumbers out. We do not have many rabbits. Wild housecats have taken toll. One morning long ago the black wild Persian stalked beneath a bush. He moved around the house, and five minutes later the yard was strewn with limp brown bodies. Wantonly destroyed, as only one was eaten.

April is an assault. Too much. Too much of everything. It begins with the toothwort, a modest flower related to the turnip. There is not much to say about it except that it is pretty and uninteresting and first. Like most wild flowers, if picked and brought inside, it droops and has a weedy negligible look, reminiscent of one's own thoughts, which seem fresh, honest, sparkling, rare, when rooted still in the cool brain cave, but in the open air, picked and presented, tend to appear dusty and weak, irrelevant to the human condition of flesh, brass, and blood.

The hillside near the creek is covered with hepatica, a lovely flower. Hepatica, meaning the liver, is an ugly name. The shape of the leaves does not resemble the liver at all. (What doctor finding a mass of flesh shaped like these leaves within the human would know what to do? What is this? These lovely green leaves? There is no liver here.)

The hillside is held up by clumps of flowers on hairy stems. The petals lavender and white and pink and purple and sometimes a rare, pale blue. The same spot of earth, riddled with moss, snail shells, ferns, oak leaves, produces this pale rainbow. They last very little longer than a rainbow, and, returning in a day or two, one finds no flowers, only hard green pods and a crop of odd-cut leaves.

These spring pools of flowers, rising year after year in the same place, are a recurring joy that never fails. It is one of the joys of living for years in the same place. This is not limited to wild land, nor to large places, but few stay long enough even on one small spot, or care enough to plant the reoccurring seed and know this seasonal miracle.

In the north pasture, the title "pasture" by courtesy only now, a pool of mint rises each spring, a lavender pond filled with bees, great bumblebees, small yellow bees, and the brown furry bees like winged mice. It is filled with the humming of the bees and the spicy smell of the mint leaves (leaves rich, green, convoluted as seashells) and the pool widens into a wider pool of white pansy violets, like a foam at the far edges. The wild pansies are separate and move in the wind.

This is the view from the woodchuck's den above the draw. His porch is well beaten down, paths lead to it under the raspberry hoops. Wrens sputter around on the ravine rocks and broken crockery from the old rabbit hutches. All this view is probably wasted on his stupid dogginess. Unless, like Pythagoras, he thinks of the violet leaves as spinach. The morning sun warms his front porch, the mists over the cool stones withdraw. I think of him coming out and contemplating this fresh April world, the smell of broken mint, the violets moving in the morning breeze, the trilling sounds of wrens before the day has brought their spirits down. But in good truth he is not emerging that early, and if it is a cold day, he is not emerging at all. He is concerned about mating, if he is through hibernating, and thereafter (four weeks to be exact) the mate has two to eight blind, hairless young.

It was time for the fat old lady to leave in late March. Holing up with any of the creatures has about lost its charm by then. The smell of woodchuck holes on warm days drives out our old dream of dozing through winter in dark woodchuck dens.

An intermittent rain this morning, now ceasing. The quail are very shrill. Soggy but nervous. The woods are still bare except for the thousand limp umbrellas of the buckeyes—a low border holding up the hill. Spent time yesterday winding up the tents of caterpillars, shoving the flabby silk masses down in the earth. They squash green. Hateful. Hateful. Slashed at briars. An enormous ache in my head. A rage against my limitations.

This delicate shaking carpet of wild flowers! Ferns, violets, squirrel corn, bluebells, spring beauties, blood-root leaves, wild poppies. All at once and together. And above the red trillium the red lilies of the papaws.

Goldfinches arrived. A mad twittering like a zoo full of canaries. Invisible. Finally saw a goldfinch separate from the gold-green tassels of the ash, the gold-green bunchy leaves. Finches seem paler close to the eye.

Rain and thunder this morning. Wish it would wash all the damn caterpillars away. They unwind in reels before my eyeballs at night. They look like phlegm on the trunks of the trees, clothing the branches. The very clouds look like their tents.

Now the sun has come out on a wet wash. The dogwood blossoms in the draw are dazzling. One drop of rain blazes up. The doves start their depressing cooing. What is the bird that keeps crying "Zooder-zeeee"? A whippoorwill last night was almost raging. Those cool, fierce calls!

The buckeye has yellow pyramids . . . thatches . . . stacks. The Ohio buckeye is *Aesculus glabra*. The extract from its bark will irritate the cerebro-spinal system of humans. (To what purpose and what end?) Its pollination is by bees. The horse chestnut is *Aesculus hippocastanum*. Alcohol from seeds is made, or can be made. The whole vegetative world is full of stuff like that. Poisons galore.

Tried to clear a path to the last great oak through the interlocking fiendishness of rusting barbed-wire fence and wood soft as cardboard. Roots of Virginia creeper vines booby-trapped the path. Old rotting tree held the old rotting fence in place. Put down the wire clippers. Came back and it had black walnut in its jaws—foraging in my absence.

This curious passion to tidy, tidy, tidy, tidy—lives . . . leaves . . . trees . . . emotions . . . house . . . surface . . . weeds . . . lawns . . . minds . . . words . . . endless sweeping, clipping, washing, arranging.

Lachesis, the measurer, was young once, a terrible young woman. The worms are unspeakable today.

What is the composition of this delicate shaking carpet of flowers, this blanket which the old king will tear away? Squirrel corn, like bleeding hearts, but waxy, white-grey-bluish; leaves fine-cut as ferns.

The honey-and-hyacinth fragrance lifts the heart. The windflower, the anemone, the wind that opens the petals, blows the petals away. The yellow wild poppy bursting from its prickly buds; the shaking bells of the Greek valerian, the bluebells. Lavender in our woods, delicate and deceptive, from *valere,* to be strong and powerful. And from its roots a drug, calming and carminative, also having tonic properties. Yellow trout lilies, white lilies, purple violets, yellow violets, white violets, and everywhere the red trillium. *Trillium sessile* and *erectum*—also known as wake-robin, toadshade, birthwort, squawroot and stinking Benjamin (and for good reason, as one knows who hunts a dead mouse or a nasty fungus smell and finds no source except this innocent and brick-red flower).

In the open fields the rich, edible leaves of winter cress, mustard or yellow rocket, *Barbarea vulgaris.* They are to be eaten on St. Barbara's day, in December, when tender, but the bitterness is too strong for most persons. Green satin shining leaves named after an early saint, "murdered by her pagan father for becoming Christian." She's turned the tables now. My bitterness is too strong for most persons. . . .

April 26.

COLD AND GREEN. COLD and wet. Chill green wet, penetrating, clammy. That's the April we know and understand. That's our April, we wet, chill, green people. Now it's gotten down to the old familiar spring. Raw, nasty, verging on frost. All that beauty out there, arranged in a big glacier. All the worms immobilized with cold. Eggs chilling in nests. Naked fledglings, utterly miserable. Frogs sinking back in the mud. Woodpeckers wet and shivering.

Just saw the bluejays stuff each other with white breadcrumbs. A chewink black and oily in the wet air. A ladderback redbelly came and gorged on damp bread. Stomach contents tabulated as Thriftway flab. Stomach enlarged by damp yeast. One is struck by the casualness of mating birds. It seems as though they had chosen a momentary perch on feathers rather than a twig.

The cold round balls of silver roll on the clover leaves. That's the old known April. The furnace booming away. The chilly dash in and out. The early maple leaves inverted like half-open umbrellas are a brown-red-green color for which there must be a one-word name.

The buckeyes have straightened out, look alive, and begin to hide all the woods beyond and below the hill.

Not one of all this vast ungrateful bird population has eaten a single tent worm to my knowledge. They pick the bare wood of the bird feeder rather than eat these loathsome, hairy, spined, nasty brown things. Things big as railroad cars, huddled in ghastly, congenial groups on the doorstep, on the rims of things. Group creatures held together by their slimy webs and webbing trails. "We must keep in touch . . . in touch . . . in touch. . . . Whither thou goest I will go. All together now. Let us bask together, eat together, spin our cocoons together in orderly rows . . . drop together . . . crawl . . . bask . . . spin." Oh, God, I *hate* them.

Observed the birds. Watched carefully to see if I had maligned them. The doves came to the wild-cherry tree—that tree whose bark is ridged and tortured like a topographical map with lines of worms. The doves' undulating shell-pink breasts shimmered. They flapped about. What think you of this for our nest? Shall we try this crevice for our yearly shamble? They do not eat the worms. A hawk sailed over the woods. He drifted and soared. It was beautiful enough to make one cry. But he ate no worms. Then came a little warbler type with big round eyes, white-circled, grey-green, black bars on wings and tail. Chubby body about the size of a green walnut. One of the unknown hundreds of birds that I will never identify. He ignores the hundreds of worms, below and around and above him. A tiny grey-blue gnat-catcher struggles with something half his size. But it is not one of *them*. Now comes a glossy cowbird. Rolls forward. Bulls up his neck. Relaxes. Points his beak skyward. The cowbird in his pointing ritual is the bird shape reduced to classic simplicity of outline. It is *bird* in art (and spiritually it is selfish essence. Dear Carol, our youngest daughter, thought to raise a cowbird fledgling and teach it how to build a nest and raise its young, thus changing the whole ancient course of cowbird life).

But at last, to our astonishment, bird and worm have met. The cowbird does it in. The balance of nature trembles back in place for one brief moment.

Brought two tulips in out of the cold. Slowly they expanded in the warmth. They got bigger and bigger every minute. Gorgeous Oriental splendor, luxurious bursting silk, exploding cool waxy fire, rose-pink, red-pink, red-carmine, red-blue, striped, veined, white-molten-red. These tulips really send one.

THE TREES ARE BLACK and cold with rain. Skies sheet metal. Yes, *this* is the right April. Not all that warmth in the beginning, all that light and perfume, all those white blossoms bulging out. Birds blasting away in the mornings, gnatcatchers *eeeeeeh* squeaking in the treetops. Cardinals cheery-cheery-cheery in the early light of mornings drilling through your eardrums like the cherubim and seraphim, and at high noon they shrilled out, "Verdict, verdict." The hawks going over, crying sweetly, mournfully, but swift—swift, as should be judgment, but never is. All that expanding revelation of the Great Mother, all that kindness, it made us uneasy. Premature paradise. There seemed to be a treacherous or reckless giving there. Made me suspicious. What was up? What was behind all this generosity? What was rising?

The old king was rising. The old waxy dying king with wet, cold fingers plucking at the blanket. Flocculating. Ah, that blanket—that soft, green, trembling, flowered blanket. Those ferns and bluebells and white trillium, that musky-sweet, honey-sweet breathing blanket of squirrel corn and rue; and all the little warm little animals lying under the leaves—little newborn rabbits and moles and even the quail chicks hatching. . . . He couldn't stand it. It was killing him.

The great cold, wet hands grew large and larger across the blanket. They could not rip it off, but they chilled it down all right. The long, wet beard and the big white hands.

AS THE WINTER MELTS slowly northward like a retreating glacier, millions of small bright balls enameled red and yellow move out from under the brown, snow-sodden leaves. From under pasture rocks or the grey-green woolly leaves of the winter mulleins, or even from attics of old houses, the bright-spotted lady-beetles, the *Sonnenkalbchen,* sun calves or Mary-beetles, move briskly out into the April light, responding to the sun and to some mysterious knowledge that their breakfast has appeared on every living twig and green shoot in the land.

Of all the two hundred and fifty thousand species of Coleoptera, the beetles with sheathed wings, the ladybird is one of the few really *good* beetles that man can depend upon to look after his interests in the savage, invisible eating war. Since the ladybird is a predacious, wholly carnivorous beetle, it has sharp mandibles fitted for the munching of living meat, and not for the slow sipping of sap or the ruminant mastication of vegetable matter. When it wakes from its long winter sleep (interrupted sometimes by the false spring alarms), it unbends its six clawed legs, which have been folded as though in death against the cold, but the ladybird does not open her eyes and scan the horizon, for her eyes have never closed and the horizon is too far for any beetle to see. She cannot even move her eyes to left and right, but the many facets of her big compound saucers are lighted by transparent windows in the hard chitinous covering that packages her body. A covering that is complete from the clubby antennae to the claws of her feet, as though one were suddenly dipped in dark varnish with only two panes for the eyes to peer through. This polished package of cuticle in which she moves will not dissolve in water or mineral acids, but, unlike the snails and clams whose rigid house makes them sluggish hearth-huggers and awkward as knights in rusty armor, the ladybug is articulated, jointed and flexible in spite of the three layers of cement, wax, and chitin that seal her from wind and rain and a generally hostile world. She has only a few short months to live her whole life (not counting the sleep) and must live it fast and recklessly, or not at all. Her glittering barrel-shaped body uses the strongest structural form, considering the limited supply of material to make it—the small and invincible cylinder that withstands all the strain she is ever likely to know.

There is not just *a* ladybug (beetle or bird), a small round bug of red, with two spots, as in the book of fairy tales. There are some *five hundred* varieties of lady-beetles, which, gathered together in a bowl, would be a mass of bright balls like a bowl of marbles, colored and splotched and spotted in pink and white and crimson and orange and black and tan and yellow, with commas and circles and parentheses, with dots, eyes, ovals, and no marks at all. There is a two-spotted lady-bug and a nine-spotted, a thirteen-spotted and a fifteen-spotted. There is the red lady-beetle, the convergent, the parenthesis, the spotted and the pitiful lady-beetle. Some are round, some oval, some one-sixteenth of an inch in length, some one-quarter of an inch. Some are red spotted with black, and some black spotted with red, as the twice-stabbed lady-beetle. There is the *Coccinella sanguinea,* who is bright red with no spots at all, and there is the *Olla abdominalis,* pale maize, almost white, and rare. There is the *Scymnus* lady-beetle, dark and small, whose larvae are covered with waxy white spines, and there is the veda-lia lady-beetle, *Rodalia cardinalis,* from Australia, whose propagation in California cleaned out the citrus orchards of cottony cushion scale within a year.

Each variety of lady-beetle gathers together with its own kind in the winter months. Thousands are huddled together, not for warmth, but to increase their unpleasant warning odor. In the western mountains they cluster by the millions, and it is from these mountain homes that the sleeping beetles are collected and shipped to gardeners and farmers all over the country to release in spring.

When the vast sleeping colonies awake, they spread out over the warming stone walls, the damp April logs, and then, without any known farewells to their bedfellows—a vast jumble of male and female bugs—spread their hard outer wings to the side, the bright shell-like elytra painted with spots, unfold their real wings, the transparent and hidden bits of hard gauze which have been doubled in two like a jointed shutter beneath the elytra, and disperse in all directions.

The thin wings beat so fast they are invisible, and carry them quickly to their first meal of the season. If the wind is high they may go a mile, or if it is windless, may drop a few feet from their home, but they cannot miss their meal, for the aphids now, by the providential timing of life, are scattered as thickly as grains of sand over the green shoots of the April world.

The rosy apple aphid, whose body has a faint, purplish glow, has emerged from eggs laid last winter on the apple twigs. She is the stem mother and will mother without difficulty from her own self-sufficient torpedo-shaped body, and without benefit of males, a host of living young. First, however, she (and they are all *shes* now in April) marches upward to the hard green apple buds, plunges in her beak, and does the best she can outside until the leaves unfold. Then she descends inside the whorl of green-grey leaves and stabs away at the stem itself and the almost invisible cluster of forming fruit. The draining of the sap stunts the leaves and they curl protectively above the mother louse, and the apples themselves dwarf and cluster misshapenly in hard little huddles.

Having no memory, no expectation of disaster, only an instinct for pleasure and for the survival of their flatulent little kind, the aphids do not expect to be devoured. Already packed and succulent with sap, transformed to honeydew, their big, foolish eyes warning them of nothing, their four sharp stylets inside the grooved beaks plunged into the leaves, happily and mindlessly they pump the sap into their bodies. They look like green paper bags full of water, and are crowded so close together the bags bump one against the other, and the smaller or later-come aphids crawl over the others and stand on their heads to find an unpunctured spot of green. They graze through their peaceful and destructive hours without even turning their heads to see beyond the herds of fat stomachs on either side. The lady-beetle, brisk and hungry, alighting on the nearest apple tree, runs briskly to the nearest leafing cluster, pinches up the nearest aphid in her jaws, and, chewing briskly, fills herself deliciously full of honeydew and masticated aphids. And the possible birth of one billion aphids is drowned in a little bug less than six millimeters long.

Even after the first attack the herd grazes quietly on, unaware that some fifty more are marked by one lady-beetle alone for that day's meal. And the next day fifty more or so, and if the weather continues mild and warm, her munching will mount to seventy, eighty, even a hundred a day, and continue on through April, May, and sometimes June. Cold damp days lay a hand on the ladybird's appetite and make her listless and unhappy, and these are great days for the aphids, who, unaffected by chill and drizzle, devour and multiply to disastrous proportion until—if they were not poisoned by man—one might almost *hear* the sound of sap draining out of the world.

Throughout the day the lady-beetle eats, cleaning her jaws and wiping away the glue (a substance far different than the honeydew) which the aphids squirt from their hornlike cornicles in a half-hearted hope to shut their devourers' mouths for good. Sometimes a large aphid will walk away restlessly from the meal, or twist and slap the beetle in the face, squirting her with its glue, or struggle too much to render the eating easy, but on the whole the banquet goes smoothly, the aphids devouring the unresisting sap, the lady-beetles the unresisting sap-balloons.

This particular devouring chain is short; the adult lady-beetle has far fewer enemies than the aphids have. The birds will have none of her. When disturbed, she squeezes a yellow and poisonous-smelling fluid from the joints of her legs, a proof, if proof is needed, of her unpleasant taste for those who cannot read red and orange, or are hungry enough to take a chance.

After a week of eating aphids and occasionally a red mite, or a nest of the cottony apple scale, and a dessert of the woolly apple aphid who looks like a bearded balloon, the ladybird feels full and maternal, and, having somewhere along the eating hours found a male—for unlike the aphid she cannot produce her young all alone—she mates, and then with renewed appetite eats voraciously her sticky manna and, cleaning her face, moves up the stem a few feet and lays her orange eggs.

By now it is late April. The wild crabs and the hawthorn are in bloom. The bluegrass, the plantain, mullein shoots, the dock and sorrel are rising. The white oaks have their first small silver leaves, and the maple tassels are washed down in the cold intermittent rains. The wild white plums have come and gone and the earth seems covered with bright, undamaged green, by fresh unbitten leaves. This is the only interval in which the uprushing green wave is ahead of the insect-eating wave. And it is a very short and precarious time. Even as the lady-beetle retreats and lays her small clutch of eggs—fifteen to thirty yellow-orange capsules all neatly set on end and crowded together underneath a leaf—all the undevoured aphids she has left below her on the branch are likewise busy. Not for them the slowly maturing eggs. The aphid mothers are all agamic and parthenogenetic, producing their living young without bother of a mate, with scarcely a break in their lifelong lunching. The pale young, expelled like tiny melon seeds, all hungry and equipped with beaks and legs, arrive in batches of up to a hundred in the week, and rapidly replace their eaten aunts. And within a week they, too, without mate or the laying of an egg, have added their own batch of leggy young to the ever-expanding colony— which, left alone, would circle the earth with a bracelet of baggy dew.

While the larvae of the ladybug still lie sealed in the orange egg, the soft stubby winged nymph of the grasshopper is emerging from the hole in the ground. The winged and dead-black mother of joint-worms is laying her eggs in the green spring wheat. The elm-leaf beetle is biting small holes in the young spring leaves of the elm and laying her eggs for the many-legged larvae who will turn much of the elm into a brown and lacelike ghost. The clown-striped cucumber beetle is feeding on weeds at the garden edge, waiting for the first tender and two-headed cotyledons of melons to arise. And the long-winged pear psylla lays its pear-shaped eggs on the end of a stiff thread-thin stalk, well in time, so that the hatching of its hairy crab-shaped larvae can take place in a white cloud of honey-scented pear blossoms and devour what is left from the feather-winged thrips who have been rasp-ing away at the pear buds from a cold, early start. And everywhere are the aphids—the clover aphids, dock and bean aphids, and cabbage aphids; pink and green potato aphids, rose aphids, peach aphids, and corn-root aphids—a vast feast of aphids feasting, and multiplying even as they feast.

Man has few friends anywhere in the insect world. Among the winged and studded, the bristling, spiked, armored, cusped and cor-niculated, the hairy and waxy, the creeping and crawling, warty and needled, the forceped and mandibled, piercing, humping, stabbing, the glabrous, oily, hairy and downy, among the whole blind and bright-eyed stubborn, swarming, instinct-driven hordes that inhabit the earth and every green living plant thereon, we can count only a small, half-hearted little band of bugs as allies. We had better treasure this little palace guard, for the enemies' name is legion.

Within six days the neat and orange capsule of the lady-egg has changed completely. Inside the tough orange shell, the chorion cov-ering (which is not chitin, though even stronger then the chitinous hides of caterpillars), the curious and methodical reorganizing of the cells has started from the single fertilized cell. With precision, like the forming of bubbles in a blown chain, some of the cells move outward to form the blastoderm; some move inward to make the mesoderm, and the future beetle larva is now covered with two cell layers and is separate from the sheltering shell.

Division and subdivision of the cells goes on, devouring the nutritious yolk and forming the intestines, the muscles, heart and nervous system, the glands and tracheal tubes. All the invisible, the complex functions of a living, predatory Thing evolve from this marching and multiplying of one infinitesimal life-struck cell.

And in six days the end result of this orderly progression, this wheeling and channeling of cells—like vast companies on a parade field magically spelling out a name—is a tiny rapacious monster, shaped like an alligator and covered with warty spines. Bearing no more resemblance to its bright jeweled parent than a slug. And apparently one miracle is not enough, and another one is due.

The beetle larva, this small six-legged monster, which looks like a series of stacked and pointed doughnuts, diminishing in size, has no compound and faceted eyes, but only a cluster of ocelli, simple eyes, on either side of its head. Each eye has only one convex lens, and so, in spite of his multiple portholes on either side, the larva is nearsighted and circumscribed to a small unchanging arc of vision, like a flashlight beam—which seems to serve him well as long as even the hind claw of an aphid comes over the edge of the arc. The segments of his body are covered with hairy warts and his color is a bluish-black, spotted with various pigments in various patterns, depending on his parent, but mainly of orange or pale yellow with four dark shining spots on his first two collars.

He emerges hungry from the egg and waddles briskly up the stem. Not inclined to cannibalism unless sorely starved, he ignores his waddling brothers, and, as though guided by the faint green sound of draining sap, finds his first aphid colony and literally latches on. Although not equipped with the long, powerful mandibles of the aphis lion, his fellow predator, a more angular alligator—who punctures the aphid, impales her and sucks out the juice, casting the empty bag aside—the lady-beetle larva has adequate sharp little jaws, a fair sense of the relative size of his meal and his strength, and in his first instar, the days between the periodic splitting off of his skin, he chooses the smallest aphids he can. This is not always easy, since he devours fifty or more a day, and so must at some time encounter being slapped in the face with a cornicle full of glue from a roused and larger aphid, but tenaciously and blindly will continue his restless and messy meal.

Four times in the two to three weeks of his larval life the spotted alligator hide will become, not surprisingly, too tight. Then the larva withdraws from the banquet table with a feeling of fullness, if not downright nausea, waddles listlessly off to some cleaner twig and the next instar of his adolescent life begins. Since the adult of an insect is anywhere from a thousand to seventy thousand times as heavy as when it hatched, and since this tremendous enlargement cannot take place gradually and imperceptibly, because of the hard shell covering in which the insect is enclosed, it must get rid of the brittle rind and bulge quickly out before the new skin hardens again and holds him in. Inside the first instar's cuticle, the varnished outer shell, a new three-layered cuticle has been forming, and when the moment of tightness beyond further toleration has come, when the last aphid that can be crammed inside has been crammed, a molting fluid pours out under the cuticle, loosening and softening the tinny armor, separating it from the tender new suit beneath. Pushing and humping, the inner man emerges, expanding like a tough bubble as he comes; and suddenly a slightly bigger, not much uglier alligator lies upon the stem. The exuviae—old clothes—blow away, and the larva's skin begins to harden until it is completely sclerotized; the endocuticle is re-formed inside the outer skin, and all is set again—until next week.

If the spring is late, wet and cold, the beetle larvae will grow slowly; their appetites fall off and the melancholy of the season leaves them weakened to fungous diseases, and easy prey for the small parasitic flies that lay eggs in their living hides. But if the spring is warm and without undue rains, the larvae will eat well and pass rapidly from instar to instar, becoming a little larger, a little hungrier, a little more useful to man with each splitting of their skins, decimating the red mites, the aphids, the sluggish and armored scales, the sluggish and cottony cushion scales.

As it nears its full growth in this stage of its life—a minute fullness of less than ten millimeters long—the larva eats with passionate attention for several days, as though cramming all nourishment it can into the alligator shape for the silent and introspective time to come. In the brief weeks of its reptile life it has plowed through some six hundred aphids, and its wandering mother, the lady-beetle, has laid a new batch of eggs every day or so while eating her own long, winding meal, and these eggs have been hatching into larvae who likewise have been devouring, so that the family eating in this one month alone is almost beyond imagination, and comparable only to what the aphids themselves have been up to.

The other predator of the aphid, the angular alligator of the lacewing fly, the aphis-lion, is busy spinning a tiny silk cocoon like a white capsule to cover the work of regeneration, brief though the period of this change may be—but the lady-beetle larva, having nourished himself into a rich and sluggish state, is not so particular or even so wise. But, depending on the immunity that has brought him well through his life thus far, he finds a place on a leaf or branch and simply stops, glues his tail to the chosen spot and proceeds to become a pupa. Some of the larvae choose to discard their larva skin in the beginning, shrugging it off and pushing it down around their tail, like a child standing in a puddle of clothes, while others retain it, partially split, and change their shape within.

By now it is late May and the second generation of lady-beetles will come into a green, flowering and swarming world. The apple blossoms are blowing downward, the apple aphids are sucking away at the young green apples, the rose-and-silver leaves of the grapes are green, and green with aphids. The huge and harmful cousins of the lady-beetle, the bean and potato beetles, striped and hungry, have begun their eating and laying of eggs on the bean shoots and young potato plants, and if not stopped will have left whole fields of pale white skeletons behind them.

In his chosen spot, glued and motionless, the lady-beetle larva begins the incredible total change, to which the changes from instar to instar are no more than the peeling of an apple skin. Here, in the space of five days or so, the whole structure of the insect thing is torn down, rebuilt and reborn.

The larva no longer eats. Not even if an aphid ran blindly across its jaws, as it might easily do—although it can move if disturbed and rear up like a snake alarmed. Its breathing slows down to the barest movement, and all its *life* is turned inward to the process of disintegration and re-forming. Small groups of cells, the histoblasts, which have been dormant within the larval form, now grow rapidly and richly, feeding on the dissolving larval cells and all the honey of the aphid bodies stored as fat. Once again, miraculous and orderly marching of cells results in a complex insect creature, now with two pairs of wings, with antennae and reproductive organs, with big compound eyes and three jointed tarsae—a creature as different in shape and appearance as was the young larva that emerged from the simple and orange egg two or three weeks ago. A precise image of the lady-beetle who laid the egg splits the parchment larval skin—and the second miracle that logic asked has arrived on punctual time.

About half of the lady-beetles born are males, which cuts their race with aphids down considerably. But if it is a female born of this first egg batch, she will begin the egg-laying cycle again, and three or four, or sometimes five, generations will complete their life cycle, their vast work of eating and procreating, before the first frost has come. Thus, if it is a fortunate year of sun, the great-great-granddaughter of the April-emerging beetle may push out the yellow dome of her egg in September—in time for an autumn meal of aphids, and then sleep. She will not lay any eggs, but eats for the winter of fasting ahead.

TOWARD THE END OF April, I went back to the clean stream, the second stream beyond the ridge. Walking to escape the war and the worms, the realization of my own eccentricity bordering on a discreet madness, walking to leave the piled, untouched desk, the paranoiac assumptions, the fears, the lethargy under which a burning engine runs. (I think of that dry pump in the cellar of the old house. The pump which turned no wheels, the leather-strap sound, the smell of burning rubber, and no water moved.) The deep pool of the polluted stream was deeper, smelled foul, looked dark. I crossed it on the algae-coated stones and climbed the hill the children called the Snail Hill where all the old snails of the world had come to die.

Beyond the ridge the silent magic came again. The spring was preserved—that spring which had rushed up in those early warm days of April. It was held here, arrested in the coolness, as in a great cave. Once again that curious miracle was manifested. A silent, waiting world of pure enchantment. A trail, not a patch, not a clump, but a *trail* of giant white trillium wandered down the slope toward the stream. Enormous green triumvirate of leaves. Beautiful, the white curved petals on long stems. Three white wax petals, three green under the green leaves—coiled and sailing as the coifs of Belgian nuns. Some curved and seeking, like the necks of swans in the search for light out of the lid of leaves. A bold height for a spring flower.

Beyond them was an unexpected shoal of wild hyacinths, their marshsedgy leaves, their tall and delicate spires, the pale blue buds, the starry open flowers—the lowest opening first, dying before the final bud has opened—pale blue with bright and brisk gold centers. A heart-stopping sight there in the shade of giant beech and hickories. The papaws had black, frosted leaves, but on higher ground the leaves were green and the blossoms hung like black tulips, carved and perfect. They are that mysterious color which is neither brown nor red nor black, but a dark shade of its own—a green-veined sable.

The bloodroot leaves had grown enormous as lily pads, and, at the roots of trees, the fiddler ferns uncoiled, pale grey-green, dry yellow scales, and the old winter ferns still beautiful, flat as crocodiles on the ground around them.

It was as silent as it had been before, in the snow. Once or twice a bird sound, the running of the stream, little waterfalls formed by a stone. The big granite boulder had small whorls of green lichen. It looked brighter, gayer, if a stone can be gay.

And then one walked into a fairy world of purple larkspur. Purple spires by the hundreds. The creek was lined as far as eye could see with purple larkspur, lined with small fallen clouds of lavender wild phlox, and ferns. There were maidenhair ferns, wiry and delicate, and fine-cut small green ferns, so close there was no space to walk between. The stonecrop was in flower with branches of white stars. A flower or fern on every inch of ground. All here, preserved and paused by cold. The upward rush of spring halted and unharmed.

The brown winter blanket of leaves was buried under a blanket of flowers. The old king was done in at last.

MAY

A cold, wet month in the main, in this year of our Lord. A green, cold ocean of leaves. Beautiful as an ocean, wet as waves. Reminds me of a month-long picnic day in Kensington Gardens. A lovely day, our hostess said; bag of sandwiches in hand, she met us at the door. Our hearts sank, our fingers froze. All day we plodded about in the freezing wind. The flowers all open and gay. Our eyes glazed with frost. Beautiful . . . beautiful, we hissed from our blueing lips.

Here, behind a large sheet of glass, we huddle and watch the margin of the woods. The day began astonishingly. Threw out white bread to the birds. Instantly materialized a huge female opossum, large and white as a polar bear. Rain-soaked, pink-nosed, she devoured the bread and humped away. A nocturnal animal at breakfast, in narrow daylight, in the rain.

Last night we heard strange sounds, like china teeth clattered together, rusty chains, tin plates. A weird calling and answering going on between invisible objects. Then a white opossum dashed across the road. An opossum has enough fat to fire five thirty-seven-millimeter shells, but I have never heard an opossum articulate before. If that is what it was.

A chipmunk comes. Noses about. Sits on a log eating something that looks like pink squirrel-corn bulbs, which are filled with the poisonous alkaloid cucullarine. He does not care. He does not collapse. He washes his nose with skinny little fingers—fast, nervous. Turns around and stares straight at me, cheeks extended.

Then falls an intermittent rain of birds.

Downy woodpecker on feeder. Wood thrush or oven-bird on ground. Strange to see them here in the open.

Red-bellied woodpecker comes. Name erroneous. Only a dry-blood streak on its belly, and a flaming red silk cap on its head. Red silk threads that shimmer.

Sparrows are singing.

Now comes the cat, Pussywillow.

A chickadee.

A tomtit. Another tomtit. They quarrel. A ball of feathers hurling to the ground.

The cat springs. The ball divides and flies away.

Bring cat inside.

Another chickadee comes.

No wrens, The wrenhouse hole's too small. Nothing but bees could get inside.

Cardinal and bluejay arrive together. That blue. That lavender. That blue. Those long Egyptian eyes!

The bluejay leaves. The female cardinal comes.

The maple leaves look glazed and sticky.

I hear the Carolinas calling.

Two downies. They look dirty. Downies always do.

Now a cowbird in the grass. Brassy, glossy, but shy.

The lady cardinal. The tomtit. A nuthatch for a change.

A sparrow. The cardinals still eating. How they Fletcherize!

A downy, a chickadee, a female sparrow. Cardinals gone . . . downy again. A monotonous coming and going of black and white birds.

Then incredibly, unbelievably, two scarlet tanagers. Like live burning coals. Black wings around red fire! Our eyeballs bulge, we grab the glasses, and shortly they are gone.

We hear they died by the thousands in New England. The sadness of that red-feathered rain, dropping from the cold skies. They could not stay in this warmer region They were programmed to go on. Driven by that which can never be revised, never unlearned, never suited to the circumstances, never tempered to the wind.

We humans have certain advantages we do not use.

Then comes the giant flycatcher, swinging out and returning to a dead limb. Crested, beautiful, in that strange blend of brown and yellow and chestnut, which changes with the light, which is peculiarly his own.

And then at last the bluebird comes. The lovely, the electric shock of blue. The heart jumps. That unearthly blue, that hue of "a color normally evoked by radiant energy of wavelength 478.5 millicrons." That's where the shocking-awake comes from. Sapphire sky. Travels through the veins like blue fire. One's struck and flares up like a dry match. Phosphorescent blue.

ON THE EIGHTEENTH OF May the air was full of flying ants. The cowbirds seemed more annoyed by the ants than interested. Then a myrtle warbler came. A splashy thing of black and white, and dabs of yellow on crown, sides and rump. (The most common of warblers, the great haughty warbler-book says. One gets the impression L. G. was in danger of being attacked by swarms of myrtle warblers, so scornful is he of its availability and ease of identity. It is not a secret discovery, like the fringed tongue, that the cognoscente can keep to himself.)

The ants began to boil out of a fence post. They streamed like smoke up in the air.

The warbler dives into the cloud. Another warbler comes. The silver wings of ants are all around them. The warblers swing and dive, flutter and perch. They discover the source of all this bounty and land on the fence post itself. They devour the ants like a pile of grey pumpkin seeds, which in truth they appear to be. The ants swarm on. What a fluttering in the stomachs of the warblers. A silvery milling about—*aagh*.

Though the horn of plenty is faltering, the air is still full of their flying. Why has no one else discovered this feast? This bright, aimless whirling? Aimless? They probably have a very specific aim. "Where's the queen? Which way? Am I too late?" Two thousand to one you are, poor little fellow, and your wings are going to drop off, anyway. Clock. Just like that. You are expendable in the highest.

The squirrels, on the other hand, continue their maddening marriage ritual one to one. The flight and the pursuit. The female is interested only in eating. The male eats nothing, but pursues, nosing her tail. He never leaves the tree. She feels free to forage in the clearing, but always returns to the tree as object of the pursuit. The game goes on and on. She manages to eat, to appear annoyed, to eat, to stay one inch ahead; to be attainable and yet never be attained. To eat.

NOW WE COME TO discuss the worms again. Year of the Worm. The apple tent caterpillar, *Malacosoma americana,* soft-bodied American.

The sun in the south, shining on a solid bank of clouds in the north, has turned them dark blue. The storm comes on fast. The bank is closing in all around. A wall of blue-grey water. Perhaps a cyclone or typhoon to solve all problems. A soft, cool drop falls. Everything's turning grey. Trees swaying. Jays getting a last choke-down of coffee-cake. Little winged bugs flapping. Now comes down the rain.

We've got a crop of evil things this year. Cowbirds, starlings, roaches, tent caterpillars—the Worms.

"They do not do well in rainy weather. . . ." Hold that thought! But they are all sitting snug in their nasty, phlegmy tents, their snotty runner webs and trails up and down the trees. They're safe. They don't give a damn for this belated rain.

Know thy enemy. *Malacosoma,* order *Lepidoptera,* family *Lasio-campidae,* whose silken roadways drape your trees. Their varnished egg nests—oh, so neat and tidy, their one-inch silk cocoons, cocoons which give off a puff of smoke if touched, which appear under the siding of houses, which are woven in socks on the clothesline, woven in grooves in pruning shears, inside of gloves, dangling from blades of grass, in the rims of garbage-can lids, anywhere, everywhere—scarcely more endurable than the loping worm itself. Full-grown, two inches long, covered with soft, light hairs, and rows of blue *eyes* along its nasty spiny sides.

"Wandering caterpillars may be trapped on flypaper. . . ." There's a laugh. No factory has wound out enough flypaper for a river of advancing tent worms. They flow, they hump in waves across the grass. They bask on the steps in the sun in herds. They keep in touch with each other. They climb the walls, they frame doors. They love circular things, they make hairy wreaths of the lids of garbage cans.

"Egg collecting contests are popular. . . ." But how about old cherry trees, tall as skyscrapers? "Many parasitic enemies . . . abundance varies from year to year. . . ." This is the third year, and they are worse than ever. They have surely done the old trees in this time. Not a leaf. Not a blossom. They look as though swept by fire.

Every worm is two hundred worms. Two hundred times two hundred equals forty thousand. Forty thousand times forty thousand . . . a little multiplying brings on despair. One generation in a year, it is said—nine months in the egg stage. Just like a human.

Now, that which had been slowly and slyly developing came to full, bold flower, and the character of this person was revealed at last. Come to flower? Come to fur. Brown and white hair big enough for a neck-piece. Rippling with horrible and steadfast intentness. So intent, its whole head seemed only one wet winking eye, traveling toward me.

WARM DAYS COME OFF and on in May. Islands in the ocean. The great rose fountain blooms with small sweet flowers. Warm heavenly sweetness in which one drifts, not drowning. Nostalgia comes. A sadness for all the lost, the unreturning summers of childhood. The cooing of the doves and the scent of roses brings it on. It's sharp and sweet. It stabs into the heart. Tears come for all the unreturning dead. For the dear aunts; for their love, for the days of summer, the long warm days of roses that would return each year, that would return—that as far as we dumb little kids could see, would return forever and ever. Aunt Mary . . . Aunt Edith . . . Aunt Elizabeth . . . Aunt Alice, oh, especially Aunt Alice. Why isn't there a heaven for such people—some reward for lovely lives, for kindness beyond imagining; some compensation for the long sickness and the long death? There's no Oakland, no family home any more. Only the cemetery, Oakhill. So snap to it and appreciate the living. Live the summers now. That's all you'll ever have. They're all anybody will ever have. Wipe the fog off your glasses and you'll see the living people around. This is their *now*. This is all there is. Be kind *now*.

IN SEARCHING FOR A bittern's floating nest among the reeds (a romantic expectation held from the days of reading Gene Stratton Porter, and revived by seeing this bird of rust-color, white stripes and covert look perched by the pond) I found, instead, a cunningly constructed red-winged blackbird's nest, made with a roof like a little house, built on a woven platform in the reeds, and the white eggs with their black scrawl clearly visible.

The blackbirds have taken over the pond—bright, beautiful and deadly. In the fall they will swarm over the cornfields, and the farmers will set out their propane cannons, and autumn will be a night- and day-mare of these monotonous explosions every half minute, circling around the hills. The torture of this sound is an accepted legal custom now. I pass my hatred of the sound on to the blackbirds. I look lovingly at the great snake who inhabits the shallows of the grassy bank of the pond. He is grey and big as a rubber tire. He weaves down through the grass, and his disappearing tail seems that of an alligator. He may be permanently stuffed from stem to stern with frogs, which explains the mystery of how so many eggs and young of the blackbirds escape him.

The winter rushes bend and break, fall down in exhausted clumps; and the young green shoots strike up with a delicate vigor among these old straw men. The old reeds creak in the wind, sink lower and gradually disappear. The cattails break off and float away, wads of soggy brown cotton.

The frogs. The unbelievable frogs, the monstrous frogs line the shore. Huge, grave and gravid; great gongs in their heads, great speckled eggs for throats, great eyes on top of their heads, great mouths fixed in smiles. Those smiles! Those great, mock smiles.

They fill the pond water. Their heads are like hippopotami in African rivers. Their sharp little hands are green leaves. Their voices are huge and ridiculous. They boom and bray. They bellow *Runnyduke runnyduke.* And some say *Newark newark,* over and over, and many cannot be translated other than *Chugarum chugarum,* as the children's books all say.

Two tiny boys come down on big bicycles. "Can we go down and look at your pond?" (The pond is on a high hill above us.)

"No, not this year."

"Why? Because of the floods?"

"Well, it's very muddy—"

"Quicksand! My, but you have big trees down here!"

"Yes, they're very big. Once they were little Christmas trees."

"How long have you lived around here?"

"About twenty-five years. How long have *you* lived around here?"

"Oh, about two—or twenty."

"How old are you?"

"I'm six, he's eight." "I am not, I'm six." "I was up at your pond once." "Was I ever up there? Do you have pets? Did your wolf run away? Do you put out food for the wild animals?"

EARLY IN MAY THE pond has drifts of white foam where the locust flowers fall and the white fluff from the willows drops and gathers. The rains keep the algae at bay, and they form green and gold islands that seem to bubble. And among the islands are the bullfrog heads, hard green boils that break the water and float, smiling falsely, hour after hour, waiting for the meal in flight.

The air smells of sweet grass, of locust blossoms, of warm water. In the shallows by the pond edge the tadpoles rise and drift in this warm water full of undigested bits of vegetative life like a slow soup. The tadpoles belly up to the floating bugs, the dragonflies arrive, but the spring is late and cold. ("Does he breathe fire?" a little boy asked. "Will he hurt me?" The name is powerful.) Transparent fish move into the shallows. Bluegills with a pale turquoise aura around them. They look tubercular. The fat pulpy faces of the tadpoles take on an evil look. ". . . at night the sharks come in from the open sea," Beebe wrote. "At noon the tadpoles come in from the open pond," I think. How can one trust such hydrocephalic things that see backwards and forwards? They are up to no good.

The reeds creak, the frogs intone, the blackbirds chuck. They can resent loudly even with a beakful of worm. A hungry young one cries; his head has a crest of downy fluff. The swallows swoop, a hawk screams, and then a cuckoo comes. Across the pond he slides in silence to a locust limb. A pool of silence seems to lie around him in the noise. His long, lovely wings lie close to his body, his long, curved beak is closed. The long tail does not move. He seems to melt into the branch.

The cuckoo's a cool bird, a beautiful bird. His eggs are big and blue, his nest a shambles. His young are covered with quills instead of down. He has been known to eat forty-seven tent caterpillars in six minutes, and I saw a pair of cuckoos in the white cherry one year eating these things, and without aid of hands they husked off the hair, and it floated away like nasty feather boas in the wind.

He's a noble bird and rare. Too rare.

Under the white honeysuckle bush a pool of white violets is still in bloom. Black-cheeked warblers and the chats come around in curiosity. I sit still, keeping a watch on my feet for caterpillars, a watch on the hole for that big doggy head of the woodchuck. A hawk flies over. Butterflies drift by. White, tiger, swallow-tail. The hole remains somber and empty. Why doesn't he come out and bask in this loveliness? I am not his view. I am hidden by grapevines. Bees swarm in the mint. Warm sound of bees in the fragrance of mint. Now comes a little plump yellow-green thing. It is a thysbe. Half bee, half moth. Over the hole arch raspberry vines, heart-shaped moonseed, and wild grape. Around it grow the crowsfeet, bedstraw and early shoots of goldenrod. What a place for a home! What a porch above the ravine. Come out, blast you, and enjoy! Be seen.

The fat wrens sing beautifully, there is the wooden-chopping sound of chat wings descending. The hole remains empty. It is getting late. I return to the cottage and there is the woodchuck sitting on the back porch, looking at me. He is the owner of many entrances and exits. He disappears.

I go home by way of the pond. Great gold frogs leaping in love or rage. Not playing leapfrog. They never make it quite over—or on top either. Ponderous. Ridiculous. As graceful as the great Dr. Samuel Johnson in a bathing suit.

". . . It is a beauteous evening, calm and free. The holy time is quiet as a nun." Some nun. The pond's a madhouse. Blackbirds frantic as a chickenhouse disturbed. *Chuckchuckchuckchuckchuckchuck*. . . . And below the frogs bellowing *Chugarum, runnyduke, newark newark*. . . . The borborygmus of the pond water, a catbird mewing *Meow meow*, the swallows still swooping, their forked tails delicate, their beaks spearing.

In the last light there was a crash in the branches of the woods, and then a terrible bird-screaming sound that went on and on in the most awful despair. I could not see anything, I could only place the sound as being from a crow—a young crow caught by an owl and carried across the stream. There was a horrible gulching sound, and the screaming stopped.

A silence followed. In the shadows I saw a wild rabbit, and thought of its loneliness in the darkness of the coming night. (He would not be; but I thought, I would, under such circumstances. All night, all life, though short, with nobody at all.)

After awhile the frogs began again. And one enormous frog sound as I left was deep and meditative. Intent, and not to be put into English words. An old Arab frog speaking.

AROUND THE MIDDLE OF May the raccoons begin to come to the house in the twilight. (The first one was wary and small this year. He seemed stiff, as from some old wound.) A raccoon's loose, baggy shape seems to change form like a hairy amoeba. Through him flow other animals, as though they borrowed for an instant that commodious grey coat, put on the black mask. Pig, cat, and fox are there; coatimundi— even at times the grizzly bear. Woodchuck he resembles, squirrel at times, but never the opossum. The first raccoon we ever saw here came in broad daylight. A female raccoon, hunching along like a little old woman in a huge shawl. She circled the house, ignored the cats. She was armored in maternity, deep in fur, hungry, perpetually hungry. She ate white bread and bacon grease. She ate constantly, ravenously. A nursing raccoon eats everything all day long. She came at high noon once and I put out food for two hours—bread, grease, table scraps, dry dog food, all went down and down. She loved sour milk and all greasy things. She literally shoveled the food into her stomach.

That was an extraordinary summer—the summer of the animals. As we learned from the Milnes' *Nocturnal Animals,* the cones and rods of animals' eyes cannot detect red light. We set up a red light outside and they ignored it as they would ignore the moonlight shining on their nocturnal paths. It seems a strange dream now—the path of red light, the bowls, and the blue plate at the wood's edge. The eyes shone in the snakeroot and the forms appeared in absolute silence. Nothing was there, and then a raccoon was there. The raccoons came first. One at a time and then two, and then four. They ate both piggishly and delicately. They licked the bowls as though devouring the clay itself. The opossums came, dirty bottlebrush opossums with pink hands, and fed on the outer circle. And the foxes came. The beautiful grey foxes. Apprehensive, wild, graceful and ghostly. One night they were all there, all at once, raccoons and opossums and a pair of foxes. Whoever sat in the plate had possession first. The opossum tried to establish rights. He rushed at the foxes and they danced aside. The raccoon left the plate—empty except for one cold potato. The opossum seized the potato in his jaws. Ran away in the night, bearing the white potato like a pearl. A firefly burned blue in the foxes' fur.

Not until June would the mother raccoon bring her young.

In a night of this latter May, I watched the margin of the woods. The animals come early on hot nights. Too oppressive in their holes. Someone had let loose a pack of hounds along the creek. They howled, barked, yodeled, looed, savage slavering sounds. A screech owl started wailing, the frogs bellowed from the pond. Night of Walpurgis, noisy as hell. And then, in the midst of this racket, a raccoon moved out into the light. Two hideous opossums joined him. Each stationed himself at a pile of food, backs to each other, and started eating, the opossums gnashing their teeth as is their custom, the raccoon quietly, deftly devouring.

They seemed mercifully deaf to the sound of the dogs, or, in truth, had gauged it exactly—sound and distance of safety perfectly measured—and then went about the business of eating on the margin of death, as is their custom. As will be the custom of all men someday.

JUNE

The small crumbling cottage was built long ago when all land was farmland in this county and, with its old ragged lilac bushes, still stands near a pond in a corner of our acres. The silver canes of wild raspberries reach across the broken windows, but the great stone fireplace is still there, untouched by time.

There is a well with a wooden windlass under a cedar tree, and living inside are hairy spiders and great black snakes coiled quietly in varying sizes. We lift up the lid and endure each other's stare for several minutes until one or the other goes his way.

On summer mornings up there, the far hills are blue, the air is warm and misty and full of white and yellow butterflies appearing and dissolving like bits of cloud. The glowing orange fritillaries, whose larvae eat the wild-violet leaves at night, and whose wings have mica spangles, swarm over the dusty pink and purple milkweed flowers, and these outrageous colors are beautiful and harmonious in the sunlight.

The high seedy grasses at the edge of the clearing suddenly

swing forward from the weight of the goldfinch gathering seeds, or the indigo bunting whose blue is like no other color on earth, the rarest, most gemlike blue, as though a wild jewel had gone by on wings.

The goldenrod is high and green, and these skyscrapers of vegetation are covered with red aphis, sucking in and out, pumping the green towers, while ladybugs devour them—choosing among their overabundant lunching lunch. Ladybug larvae and the delicate lacewing also devour. The aphis jerk in and out, in and out. The harvest spiders stroll and loll. And an unknown, evilish thing, humpbacked and spiny-legged, crawls up and pauses at the red bubbly fountains.

We have this clearing around the cottage under control now, although this was not always so, and the grasses five feet high, with seed heads on them like busbies, grew up to the door. We no longer need old Tom Sayre with his scythe, like Father Time. Old Tom is more than eighty and moves slowly, stiffly but relentlessly, weed-destroying through his days. I have never seen him still. He hates all weeds, and he walked two miles in the early-morning mists to chop ours down, his great scythe moving for six hours, as though a pendulum had been set in motion and could not stop. He is a healthy man, and though he chews tobacco, he never drinks, and has been known to warn that "lips that touch liquor shall never touch mine"—although what brought this on is hard to say. He is a craftsman and wants to see a job well done. But when he had cut slowly and methodically westward through three days of cocklebur and narrow dock, we felt we could not afford a pathway to the rim of the world and told him it was time to stop. He paused and regarded us with thoughtful scorn. "You're a couple of tightwads," he said. "I ain't anywheres near done."

But misers or not, we had to let him go; and he went back to trimming his own yard to bark and bone. Months later I met him in the grocery store and said hello. He peered at me without recognition. "Who the hell are you?" he asked. A greeting not wholly lacking in friendliness.

"Don't you remember me?" I said. "You cut our weeds up by the pond."

He nodded absently. "You're better-looking than you used to be," he said, and stumped away with his groceries down the center of the road.

Once the clearing was made, the children played up there more often, and, on the long stone and concrete slab that was the back porch, now cracked and punctured by pokeweed and grapevines, they made three little stoves out of the fallen chimney bricks and made real fires and cooked real food and held long and very real conversations. It was on one of these expeditions that they saw the fox vixen running from the rubble that used to be the cellar door of the cottage, one of the exits from the underground tunnels where this year the woodchucks live.

Oddly enough, although I have lived most of my life in the country, I had not until recent years seen a fox close at hand—once, running from the hounds, and once at dawn, grey as the cold mists from the pond, floating lightly over the brush heaps by the barn.

The fox seems fast and fearless, clever and cunning, and without manners or morals or scruples, a legend of freedom, and I had long found release in this private image in my heart. When harassed by those affairs of life for which I am not well fitted—those which require grace or authority, political acumen, wit and social ease; weddings and meetings, funerals and gatherings; or when, bewildered by the constant domestic matters where the warm maternal wisdom and patience are drawn on as though they were from an unfailing spring, instead of a cistern much in need of rain—then, tormented by conflicting voices, by inadequate responses, by lack of wit or wisdom (or even the answer to Who-the-hell-are-you?) the self sought relief in the heart's image of the wild free fox. The fox on the ridge moving lightly, seeing far below her the hound on the chain, the old, slow, doorstep hound, whose eyes followed only the boots and the shoes and the beetle's tracks. The wild red-and-grey fox circling the farm lots, free, running the ridge, regarding with cold amber eyes the penned white flock, or sleeping in the silence of the ferns.

And so, when the children had reported seeing the fox twice, I took to going up at odd hours and sitting patiently on the cistern lid of the back-porch pump and watching the dark, dry hole that led back to the den. Hole watching is not for many souls. "Let's go," Carol used to whisper in two minutes. "The animals *never* come out!" (But last year the woodchucks *did* come out. They were very loud and clear. You have not really been whistled at until a woodchuck has whistled at you. The shrill warning whistle of a marmot is of poignant rudeness. It goes right through the ear and pierces a hole to the other side. Nor is it well to come between one and his burrow, or he may clamber over you in his rush to reach the warm, smelly sanctuary of his home.)

I was watching alone on a late June evening, having come up to put behind me various unsolved problems, probably insoluble, various choices, equally unchoice, and in the coolness I sat on the cistern's edge and waited. The children had been using the pump, and the smell of wet concrete splashed by cistern water, the sound of water dripping back down in the darkness, brought back the summers of my own childhood, the memories of Arcadia in June. A chipmunk came and ate the last cherry on the little cherry tree. The yellow chat began his mad, dissonant song and then, suddenly folding his wings upward like a butterfly, parachuted downward, legs dangling, singing, and was gone. Little brown toads sat on the bricks and slowly turned brick-color. The air filled with the scent of the great lace elderberry blooms, an odd off-scent, not musk, part lily. The young red-bellied woodpeckers were around in the walnut. They have no red at all on them in this stage but are the color of bleached driftwood. The old-grey feathers of the young.

It was very quiet, and there was no sound from the hole, but a movement flickered, and then a small grey fox came out, awkward and curious, neither the fuzzy baby young, nor yet half grown. And then the vixen was there. Her long neck arched above the cub's head, and then there were two more cubs, and they moved behind her, out from the tangled grapevines to the open grass. She was very beautiful, grey-red fur behind her ears, and the grey fur running down into red below, and the plumed tail fringed in white. She moved forward to cross the clearing, and the three young foxes started to follow her. It occurred to me that this was the final evening for their cottage den, and I had barely come on time to see them before this home was abandoned and the hunting lessons began.

Then she saw me and froze. We looked at each other and she moved her head just once, backward toward the young foxes, who retreated under the house. A long, slow growling that seemed to come deep out of her body began, and was a continuous flow of sound, a very low and frightening sound.

I did not move at all, and we stared into each other's eyes for what seemed a long, long time. I was afraid. Her eyes were cold and amber, and once, perhaps from the gnats, she let the lids droop down. There were ticks in her ears, and one ear was bitten and ragged on the edge. The sound in her throat went on and on and I thought of moving backwards, then did not move at all, and only returned her chilly stare.

This silent confrontation without communion came finally to an end. The growling ceased, the fox simply turned away and trotted off into the snakeroot and was gone. She did not even look back to see if the cubs were out of sight. She had decided I was not a dangerous thing, and she had the night's hunting still to do. I was dismissed and felt very grateful and somewhat shaken. There had not been much distance between me and that delicate sharp muzzle. I did not really feel I had outstared her. She had decided when the meeting should be done.

I turned and came home. In the long looking, I had seen her as she really was—small, thin, harried, heavily burdened—not really free at all. Bound around by instinct, as I am bound by custom and concern. And so, although I saw the grey foxes again that summer coming close to the kitchen door at night for food, the heart's fox vanished forever that evening in the woods. And that winter a hunter trapped and killed all the foxes of these woods and fields for miles around.

ALL DAY, A RAIN of life and death goes on. A catbird crashed against the pane and fell gasping. Then it gathered itself together in a narrow canoe shape and lay there patiently waiting to recover or to die. Awareness is a name for agony. I wish there was something to pray to for its life. But one must not get excited. One must not grieve. Nature, Mom, all-powerful, monstrous and monolithic Mother sits and chooses.

My birthday is coming up. Fifty-seven years. Hard to believe, I feel new each day. New ailments. New worries, new thoughts, new attitudes. I grow here and there—send out weird shoots, adventitious roots. Remain sane. O, coldly sane. I cannot budge this great rational core. Can't con it into anything. Don't you want to live a little before you die? It doesn't move.

I am sick of war. Every woman of my generation is sick of war. Fifty years of war. Wars rumored, wars beginning, wars fought, wars ending, wars paid for, wars endured. When I was seven we entered the First World War, and since then my lifetime has spanned a half-century of wars. My husband was in the war for four years. My son has served two years as a conscientious objector. We who are opposed to war know what all the frustrated of the world must feel. The war is escalated degree after degree after degree. Unannounced; denied; discovered; done. We know the frustration of the conference, the delay, the vague promises. The opposition, the monolithic opposition, the misinterpretation, the prison sentences, and the silence. The deaf old ears, the immobility, absolute and final. And this is what the young black men feel, a thousand times over. This is where the fire and the gasoline bombs come from. The broken glass and the burning.

How much can you absorb by eye and ear and flesh, and live? Crisis after crisis, trouble, sorrow, disaster, sickness. The very fact of this constant knowing tempts one to deny the brotherhood of man and the fatherhood of God. Enough is enough.

A great, triumphant cry of self is needed. The will to live, and to have life more abundantly. To stop killing and being killed, for the old men and their mad old fears and their musty old way of life. To stand up and say no.

And if some morning all the middle-aged men and women of the world should wake and say, "I will not pay for the killing," the beginning of the new world will indeed have come.

In the meantime, pacifists lead a lonely life. Not even gathering together can take the place of that vast, warm sun of approval that is shed on motherhood, on law-abiding, on killing, and on making money. Someday will we come into our own? Well, motherhood may move into the shade. Law-abiding is going through a trauma, But killing and making money are good for a long, long time.

THE ESSENCE OF JUNE is the wild grape in bloom, is the honeysuckle and the daisies. And this year, I am aware for the first time of the powerful, musk-sweet smell of the ailanthus. That tree which grows like grass everywhere, anywhere, and could not die out if it wanted to. The white and purple beardtongue blooms, there is a quietness in the air, the heat begins and the cuckoos call.

Morning and evening odors fill the air, willows and warm water, warm yellow blossoms, sweet grass, sweet grape. The mother raccoon comes once again in the afternoon, large, grey, with black formal paws held stiffly aside when not clutching at the food. Then that night she brings her young.

The mother comes first, warily. Her head rises, peering over the bellflower, half hidden by the wild-lettuce leaves. Fireflies sparkle around her foxy face. Then she is there in the open, under the red light—no transition, no sound, just there. And suddenly she is surrounded with little fur shadow balls. Little raccoons with big ears and big tails. They glide, they roll on invisible feet, they plunge into the bowls up to their necks. They eat as though they would never eat again. They run from bowl to bowl. Sometimes the mother drives them away, sometimes she lets them snatch food from under her nose. She hears something and stands up on her hind legs, stretches surprisingly high. The young rush and cluster around her, a furry pyramid. Then she drops down and eats again. They all eat. Little white moths flutter through the grass. (I know them. I know them well. They look white only in the darkness . . . *Malacosoma* has hatched all over the place.) She brushes a moth away from her nose. Something moves in the bushes. Another raccoon prowling. She growls and rushes. She will not tolerate anything coming near her precious young. Not even old children of last season. There is nothing more ferocious than a raccoon fight, a family fight, for they are a mass of relationships for miles around. Later in the season the opossums will come and eat with them—young raccoon, young possum, with their heads together in one bowl. But now the ghostly rat shapes move warily around the rim of light. And there won't be anything left when the raccoons leave.

This is the high point of the summer, this gathering of little wild things in the pool of light. The little voices of the raccoon young are curious trilling sounds. A musical chirping as of a nest of birds. Their little fur shapes, their small black hands and bright eyes, their wildness and their innocence nearly break your heart. They come and go so swiftly it is almost as in a dream, but this is the measure of a thing's true wildness, this is the only way we know it is real.

JULY

Skies, fields, ponds, a mass of redwing blackbirds. Saw a hawk laboring over the fields, covered by a cloud of blackbirds. His head in a gnat-ball of birds. Where did all these flying things come from? These blackbirds flocking suddenly. Noisy and restless. Wave after wave over the pond. The trees full as monkeys in a jungle. How sweet we would have thought that domed nest in another spring. But not this time.

Armies of bullrushes are taking over the pond. Moving out toward the center, pushed forward by the willows. Tried to cut some of the willows with a corn knife. The old branches clanged like steel. The new ones gashed open like white-throated snakes. I'm a lousy cutter. The big frogs are sluggish on chilly days. Almost stepped on them. The purplish-black dragonflies are huge. Their wings have a fierce metallic sound. Gathered cattails for our little friend, the stocky, very small little boy who comes down to visit. "I am a *professional* swimmer," he said. "I caught a fish once that was *probably* a shark." He was proud of his new sandals, very leathery and strappy. Once he came alone very late in the evening. "I came to see you," he said, "because there was nobody else to see. Nobody on my block was allowed out." He spent a long time arranging the cattails to stick out like rockets behind his bike. He looked at the flowerpots on our cistern top—our instant patio. "You would have a nice backyard," he said, "if you had a swimming pool in it." He punctuated all his sentences with the name of God, like periods and commas. His family is large. Extended by his confusion of cousins with sisters and brothers. He did not smile often, but when the smile came it was very sweet and broad. He was a square little package of brightness and life, and we felt bad when he said he was going away to live in Kentucky. No more professional swimmer on the doorstep. No more advice.

TODAY IS WET, DAMP, soggy and swollen. My fingers are swollen. The air is swollen and warm. The butterfly wings are swollen. The wool rug is big with water. It is rising off the floor. The furniture is getting enormous, fat and undulating with water. Everything sticks. Is up tight. My brain is a big sponge. It rises against the skull. It will pour through the fontanel.

The far hills are covered with blue mist. The blackbirds sound like a rush of rain. They are pests. I hate them and all their speckled young. A breeze tries to move through the soggy air. The leaves let down the gathered rain.

Sun comes through the sog. Makes everything ten times worse. Thank God the house is clean. The wet and dirty clothes fought down into the cellar (where they soak up damp and grow enormous, ectoplasmic forms—cloth dough). My stomach swells and invades my throat. My feet are getting bigger and bigger. Overflowing the sticky leather shoes. Even my hollow heart is heavy. Brain, heart, feet, all sponge. I weigh a thousand pounds this morning.

The grass loves this world swamp, this massive aerial soup. You can see it grow before your eyes. The pine trees reach the house, flop down exhausted on the roof. Their great, green, bristly arms embrace us. The rain from every needle rolls down the roof.

The sky is grey. It is mashing the swallows low. Something is pressing the grief button. Tears are appropriate. Toads swell with fear and rage. They swell with rain. Their soft, fat throats vibrate. Their gold-rimmed eyes have no expression. They have horns on their toes.

Down under the ground the moles are *expanding*.

ALL THE WARM HONEY things, musky things flowering, the dusty, musky milkweed balls, the honey-sweet buckwheat vines remind me of summer nights riding past fields of flowering buckwheat in Columbia, Missouri.

Aunt Laura died on the fifth of July, at three in the morning. Ninety-three years old this month. The last of the Franklin sisters. It's all over now. Everybody's suffering is over now. There was no joy for any of them at the end.

This is one of the years of the Vietnam war, this is one of the years of the black revolution. This is one of the years of the Israel-Egyptian war.

A move has been started to educate the poor to file bankruptcy claims. A splendid idea. Start new again. Break out of the whole rotten coffin.

Two white butterflies go by the window. I must get out. Out! It's a panic. I can't stand the walls. You haven't a character vigorous enough to panic. You are just sitting there. You lie a lot.

I feel tired and heavy and without grace. Without grace of God or flesh, or mind.

I shall file bankruptcy of another sort.

IN THE WALNUT GROVE, whose leaves are gold in the evening light, the blue bellflowers are beginning to bloom, tall and delicate spires along the path. And the small blues, the butterflies, open their mini-wings that alternate blue and grey like dusty jewels. A bit of fudge hops in the path, a toad traveling. The path is a delight. Broad and covered with small leaves, second growth of thimbleweed and clover, close to the ground. Each leaf like a flower, so that one walks on a delicate carpet, winding through the grove under the thin trees bordered with bellflowers, and emerges into the sunlight of the pasture.

Blue is rare in nature. Sky and sea have most of it. True blue is hard to find on earth. Most of what's called blue runs off into the purple. But there's the bluebird, a piece of sky. The indigo bunting of unearthly dark vibration. No color like it. No mineral, no jewel. There's the bluejay, whose big bold blue is muted by the black leading which holds his panes of sapphire glass in place. There are the dark-blue seeds of wild grape, almost black. The big round balls of moonseed vines, dark blue and shiny. There are the hanging blue balls of the Solomon's seal in autumn, dark as wild grape. Blue seeds of sassafras trees held in scarlet cups. Once I saw a cerulean warbler. So high up, so far away, that only once the blue shone through the opening of green leaves. But I'm positive of it. There are the blue eyes of chalky blue-green dragonflies. And in summer mornings, drifts of blue along the road from chicory flowers. But here we start creeping into the lavender, the true blue fading; the wild hyacinths aren't really blue, we start calling violets blue, pale wild pansies rising to purple, rich, shining purple in the wild larkspur flowers. And the whole field of purple broadens out and carries one away. There's no end to this purple. Color is a strange thing. I always loved purple as a child. Purple velvet. Purple pansies. Now all its variations disturb me. With sunlight coming through it, or in the dark woods, the larkspur is beautiful. But only there. (Larkspur is poison, those fat lively seeds are deadly. Staphisagroine. Death in the fine-cut leaves.)

In the pasture, only a name now for this open piece of land beyond the walnut grove, the wild bergamot fills the air with its warm mint smell. It is lavender with no pretense of blue. We had red bergamot once, the domestic relative of this wild pasture. Bee balm, enormous, like Fourth of July explosions. A peculiar red, neither crimson nor luminous. A wood red. The dazzling eyes of blackberries are there. Polished and abundant. Thorny and sharp and acid. Gathered a cup for Grant and was raked by those tiny little thorns, bitten from head to foot by a world of insects, in five minutes. The teasels are high and crowned with purple flowers on their brushes, surrounded by long green horns, like Texas steers. They grow higher than my head, and hum with bees.

I am feverish and irritable with chiggers. Toads have chiggers, too. A fresh approach is needed to the chigger. Where to begin? The chigger is one one-hundredth of an inch long. His poison spreads into a lump a thousand times bigger. It rises into a red loaf of flesh. But he, the chigger, is bright yellow and blind. He runs swiftly, apparently sniffing the air for flesh, or, hopefully, to encounter edible objects. A large mass moving through the grass is a great flesh-fall for the chigger. He likes the base of a hair follicle and, perching upside down, buries his beaky face and hangs on.

It is said that he drops off in the autumn, lies dormant in the soil—no, not dormant, but molting. Two or three weeks are spent as "quiescent nymphs," then they molt again and become adults. Still they sit there anyway, adults, quiescent, until spring. Then—and here the record becomes confused and cloudy—ten months are spent in adult stage. Adults do not attack man. Adults lay eggs. Eggs hatch, and what hatches normally lives under the overlapping scales of snakes, or on land turtles. Or on rabbits. Why, then, all this scurrying rapidly about to find man? What's the matter with the cool scale of a snake? The slow ride on a turtle? The long, germy hair of a wild rabbit? That expression, "normally lives," needs explanation.

Metcalf and Flint write of the chigger: "If one anticipates a visit to the domain of these small tormentors, almost complete freedom from attack can be obtained by treating the clothing with dimethyl phthalate, dibutyl phthalate, or benzyl benzoate."

The whole midwestern world is his domain.

BELOW THE NORTH PASTURE the creek water is a strange, evil, salamander green. Its winding snake course is marked by the winking silver bubbles. Right . . . left . . . right . . . left . . . spiraling down to the river, carrying its load of waste to the sea. Lift the green algae with a stick and they come up in heavy green nets and veils.

The gnats dance in front of my eyes. They use my eyeballs for a mirror and dance for their own delectation. They do not light, but they drive me crazy. Twigs crack in the wilderness of green, but nothing comes.

The maidenflies open four black velvet wings. The dragonflies of this pool are black and milky blue. The stream flows over beautiful stones, past green thickets of horsetail plants, a miniature forest of fir trees. The only sound is the crisp-paper crackling of the dragonfly wings, and then a kingfisher rattles. I sit very still. Something seems to be coming up the creek. A soft sound. Then I feel the wind. It blows the gnats away. It sways the stems, and the bodies of maidenflies—the electric-blue bodies, the turquoise green. The coming of a breeze on a still, hot day is an awesome, lovely thing. One finds oneself praising God against one's will. The relief! The marvel of feeling well again.

The kingfisher comes to rest at last. On the same log where I am sitting. What big, beady, sharp, stern eyes he has. What a beautiful speckled ruff—and that vibrating fan, his crest! In the shadows, his blue had a greyish cast, his red, the red-brown of dry blood. He kept up a constant trilling. Is he trying to scare up the fish? He dived with a splash, returned frowzy wet, crest dripping. He swallowed the minnow and shook his wings. Feathers awry—rust, blue, white, every which way. A great squat bird. A marvelous bird. He honors our small polluted stream.

This fallen tree, this maple where the kingfisher perched on the end above the pool, is not dead. Its roots dig deep into the bank, and two young branches have turned into trees, upright, simple and sturdy maple trees, such as one sees in new subdivision streets, growing out of the prostrate body that hangs above the stream.

The viburnum is in bloom; all up and down the creek is the warm, sweet smell as of plum blossoms. And here is a clump of pickerelweed, that great, lush, shiny tropical green which seems suitable for the African waterways—and for this stream. Its bloom and seed is a green cloud, a big gnat-ball of delicate little things, both coming and going.

Patience pays off. Silence and stillness bring reward. (Nothing moral about it, but it's the only way you'll ever see anything but green vegetables and bugs.) At the far end of the pool something slipped into the water. Something bigger than a frog in broad daylight moving around among the rocks. The raccoon was fishing.

(Where are all your animals? the little children cried, running, shouting, through the woods. Twenty little children, panting, shouting, screaming, throwing rocks into the streams. Birds, frogs, even bugs went rushing to the hills. How sad that they thought they might see what only hours of silence, days of watching, ever bring to sight. They liked the water. They saw a bird or two. They found green walnuts. "They smell like lemons," they said. They were afraid of snakes they never saw. One little girl put her tiny dark hand in mine. She did not want to walk in the woods alone, but she wanted to be there. "We could get a little bag, if you had one, and come back later all alone," the little girl whispered, "and pick up the walnuts all by ourselves." Children should have greenness. There should be parks of greenness everywhere. This is a mad world of roads and concrete blocks and people going somewhere else because they can't stand to be where they are, because they've ruined where they are, to get somewhere else which is ruined, to come back to where they were. There should be parks for people, and woods for animals, while there is still room on earth for both, and time. Put the parks back in the cities where the people are. A park every block. That's not too much. That is as important as eating and drinking, for the body and the soul. What kind of life is it to live on the edge of a concrete street, four lanes, six lanes wide?

What kind of a neighborhood is a neighborhood of streets and cars and cars and streets? Not all the plumbing or the new paint in the world can make that into a neighborhood, or into a life.

The raccoon was fishing. He fished as though he did not really want to get wet. Sometimes he hopped with his tail high, as his hands pursued his food under the water. He ate whatever he found right there in the stream. He rested his chin on a rock and felt underneath it, brought up a dripping crawfish and ate it right there in the stream; green water dripped from his fur. He came downstream, zigzagging along the margin. He ate several times, then slowly, dreamily, climbed the bank. He saw me, or saw a silent alien thing, and paused and stared. I did not move. He stared, I stared. He moved away and climbed a tree. There he stopped in a crotch and dried and cleaned his fur, pausing sometimes to look down at me with a wondering, idle peer. He seemed sleepy, and after awhile he climbed higher and disappeared.

The sun is high and hot. A single yellow jewelweed blossom, large and pale yellow, not orange like the jewelweeds in the pasture and the draws, dangles above the stream. A hummingbird zooms and sizzles through the flowers. The propeller wash of his wings shakes the whole plant from stem to stern. Mulleins along the stream have reached their peak. Spires plastered with pale-yellow blossoms, pale-green and hairy leaves flopped out. Gold coral fungus grows out of old stumps. One could go about gathering an enormous yellow bouquet out of the heart of July. Fill the arms with orange lilies, the ubiquitous gold; sweep up the sunflowers, the gold honeysuckle, the great stalky suns of compass plants and prairie dock; find clumps of black-eyed Susans rimmed with gold, and wild coreopsis, ragwort and squawweed through the high, dry woods, yellow hearts of daisies and bed-straw in the fields.

Gold bugs, yellow butterflies, orange lilies. What to do with this great fragrant glow? Well, hold on to it. You'll want it in the days to come.

AUGUST

August began with a wild, tormented braying sound at one in the morning. An enormous trumpet of cattle sounds under the windows. And into the yard light came a big red cow with delicate, fierce horns, pouring out this sound like a lost soul. (As well she was, poor doomed thing.) She ran on into the darkness, and other shapes poured after her—white steers keeping close together, in the way of lost cattle.

Early in the morning, when the valley was still dead white with fog, a motley crew of men and boys, one armed with a rifle, came following the tracks sunk deep in the ground. They were hunting the cattle escaped from the slaughterhouse. In an hour they were wringing wet with sweat and weary, but somehow they had gathered and driven the cattle down the road, unkilled before their hour, cattle being strangely dull herd creatures.

When the men were gone, my sister and I made an expedition to the junction of the streams. Fortified with jars of water, graham crackers, and my nephew, who is nine, we set off to reach the blue clay cliffs, and the far, pure stream, but Brian preferred the broad creek full of sewer-fed green slime. He liked the running water full of jolly detergent bubbles and waving fronds of algae. Here the slime algae direct the course of the water as much as the stones do. The stones low in the water and gravel are black with old, oily algae. One could try to imagine them as volcanic stones. But this doesn't go far. The monstrous growth of algae is like the growth of people. Swelling, multiplying, seeping and clinging.

A red-striped snake slid under the green. A candy stick gone snake. There was a raccoon print in the mud, and the water spiders skimmed backwards and forwards on their snowshoes, making a maddening dance that seemed to have a pattern but did not.

The big pool was full of sunken algae gardens. The sun's big eye banged back from the water. The mud was brown and undisturbed on the rocks below.

A locust sizzled, and leaves fell with deceiving sound, as of an animal coming. The rocks deceived, too. One stood rounded and upright down the stream, like a mother otter clasping her otter child in webbed hands. Jutting low rocks looked like muskrats. Brian liked this creek with its waterfalls and its feeling of something happening, or about to happen. Its giant beaver dams of fallen logs and trash. He found a very good golf ball and a fine rubber tire. The great polished leaves of the water plantain gave it a feeling of Africa. Were I nine, I would have agreed with him. A golf ball would have been Leakey's early man.

But he is also a rock hunter, a fossil hunter, a collector. A new wind comes with him. He is seeing and thinking things for the first time. And later, even as he sat morosely in a cold, shallow pool of the pure creek, sat and sat and got chilled, waiting for the old people's love of the pure and unpolluted to run down, he gave off beams of newness—vital energy, like radium, in the green decaying woods.

This far creek had shallow pools connected by thin trickling streams. A papaw leaned across the creek bed, and its head was heavy with silver-green fruit. Five perfect papaws within the sweep of one's hands. Doubtless the wild things come at night and count them. Sniff the pale coming scent. Wait.

Emerald beetles flashed on the stones. The great granite boulder sat in thin, running water, a dull rose color, flecked with green moss and lichen and sandy quartz. The repose of stone! It lays a silence on our mouths and minds.

The ferns are green, still, the bloodroot leaves gold fans. The smell of fungus rises when old logs are disturbed.

On a stone in the sun there was this butterfly. Closed like a book, its wings were dull reddish-grey. Then it opened them. Holy God! It glowed like an orange, fiery coal. A suffusion of light. Red, orange, orange-red, melting down into edges of red-violet and pure blue.

Then it snapped its burning pages shut and the light went out.

THE GUNS—THE PROPANE EXPLOSIONS—GO all day long to drive the blackbirds from the cornfields. Once I called the Novitiate, which owns the nearest farm. I said the sound was driving me mad. The father said he was new here. He did not know about the shooting. I said no one—no human—was shooting. It was a thing. He had a sad voice. In half an hour the thing was turned off. A great peace descended. You cannot imagine the difference. The silence!

The next day they began again. I did not say anything more. It is appropriate that we should listen minute after minute to this mechanical firing, so that we do not forget even for one minute that there is a war. A war that has grown hour by hour into terrifying and monstrous proportions. A creature insensate, devouring, destructive of all values and all humanity. A Thing that will turn—that *has* turned—upon its reluctant parents and its insane midwives.

The sourness from the sound is a permanent part of my blood now, whether it's there or not. I have terrible dreams. I don't sleep well.

THE HIGH MARK OF this month came late in August. At two in the afternoon of a hot, green day. Where the two creeks join, pure and polluted becoming one, I saw a black shape run across the stones. A shape like a drowned black cat. A mink. I sat down on a stone and waited. My eyes like big, burning headlights fixed on the spot where it had been. Two minutes passed, and then another little dark shape came from the wet weeds. Dove into the water, rose and climbed upon a rock. A small brown mink, shaking off the water. Every hair with silver water seemed visible to me. And then it was gone. Under the yellow jewelweed the grass was flattened.

After that, a vision never quite believed, I went down again and again and waited for the minks to come. Did incantations. Waited, suffered my head in a gnat-ball. Thought of the little Ozark boy who "got his head caught in a gnat-ball. Never been right since." ("Never been right since" . . . what difference does it make? Never *was* right.) The gnats rimmed my glasses. If one keeps still, plays dead, they go away, as, it is said, go grizzly bears. It was warm and cool. Jewelweed yellow and orange, higher than my head. A great big hummingbird came. Swollen with honey or something. A great yellow butterfly came. Larger than the large hummingbird. Or have the gnats distorted my vision? No mink. No mink today.

Moved away. Went upstream to the old perching log above the wide pool. Here the stream is beautiful, a gold-brown with violet shadows, and wide blue patches of reflected sky. Green algae islands hold up a frog. Thin, delicate dragonflies or damsel flies without the black velvet—the *Coenagrionidae,* not the *Agrionidae* (the family name sounds like a mouthful of gravel), order *Odonata,* species *Ischnura.*

Something is making wide countercurrent circles in the pool. Something is moving this way. A dark narrow shape. Is it a stone? No, it moves. It noses toward the bank. Our prayers are to be answered. A mink is coming. . . . The shape emerges, humps along the weeds, gathers green stuff, has a long, long tail that is hairless. Our prayers are not answered. It is a muskrat. We cannot even pretend it is a beaver, although it has a beaver face. (A beaver left over from the glacier's retreat?) That tail deceives no one. Well, a muskrat's something new. I've never seen a muskrat on this place before. It's a wild thing. Its broad back, as it paddles away, green weeds mustached on either side, is pleasant, and its tail is out of sight. Suddenly it dives down with a *choink* sound. Disappears. It is stuffing its home under the bank.

Walked two hours in the rain, soaking up the silence of the guns along with the water. Heard an odd rushing sound as I came near the open field. The sound of insects singing through the water of the rain!

The great rock was washed slowly clean by the slow rain. Leaves fall on its lichen flowers. Its colors of brick and brown and rose-green bright in the grey light of the rain. Invisible birds sang. Everywhere the leaves moved, rippled, twitched with rain. In the woods the drops select or pass over. I grew wet very slowly.

Looked down, and there were the little eyes of August. Wild leek eyes. Circles and clusters of bright black beady eyes on a tough thin stem. A pleasant shock. A surprise. *Allium tricoccum* along the ridge path where it comes down and wanders away in the woods. They are neat and brisk. The size of pinheads. The hard, bright seeds bounce. I always miss their hour of flowering, see only these bright black eyes. They see me first.

In the muskrat pool the falling drops made bubbles and circles. Teacups in saucers, if you will. Until the whole surface of the pool was covered with these silver circles and white, winking bubbles. I sat above the muskrat hole and looked down. Could not see him. Then, there he was. Swimming downstream, bearing in his mouth weeds that grow only a long way up the creek. He looked like a wet hay wagon. He appeared to melt into the mud along the creek bottom.

I grew cold and wet waiting for his return. Shoulders hurt from the damp. Enough. Coming back, the wet pasture was a strange, misty heaven. Rain on the wild mint and the greening goldenrod. The cedars were wet with rain. Gold and red buckeye leaves falling. Buckeyes prickly and gold. Purple bergamot is fading and thistles coming. I listened to the sound of trees.

All through the woods, dead trees lie in the arms of relatives or alien bystanders, there when they fell. They make strange sounds. No, familiar sounds, in truth—familiar to me. The sound of saddles creaking. That sound at night on the long, warm roads in Columbia. Riding in the darkness past fields of flowering oats and barley. The steady creak of the saddle leather.

These trees creak even in small winds. Some chide, or low like cattle. Some sound like the beating of bird wings. Some, less tightly lodged, chirp and sing. Two great trees on the hill groan with the iron sound of chains moving. One would not wander a strange wood in the night. Not a wood full of lodged and embracing trees like ours.

The worst sound of all is that chicken sound of brooding. An old tree caught in the arms of a young one. In the wind, one cannot tell which tree it is that invokes the sound.

All paths on this steep place are up or down. The path through the walnut grove is a carpet of tiny plants. Not flowers; *plants* like flat green flowers. Lily pads of mint leaves. The path sprouts little toads with bright eyes. Their soft hands grasp at blades. They are awkward and frail. Lovable.

Things are green, for August. By things I mean snakeroot, grass, various shrubs, and so on. Out of the things flew catbirds and thrashers, and the tree heights were full of the rushing sound of starlings.

Around ten o'clock at night the mother raccoon comes now, in August. The three young ones follow with their peculiar hurried gliding pace. The young ones eat frantically, holding the dish quiet with one black hand. Their ears have grown, their little faces seem more foxlike. Their white ears prick above the furry balls of their bodies. The bushy tails are plumes. The mother is impatient with them now. She wants to eat alone. They won't leave her alone. She snaps at them. They snap at each other. They are never filled.

An opossum comes to the empty bowls when the raccoons go. It has a face like a sharpened pencil. Body a hairy insect. Humped and horrible.

August nights are cold. The fields full of fireflies. White moths flying low in the grass. Skies full of white stars. They seem no different from the summer nights of all the years before.

I woke one night, got up and went to the window. Looked down into the darkness. Down, down the steep darkness into the creek below the hills. Had a vision of the little muskrat plying back and forth, back and forth, in the cold night water. Making a winter home, and the world closing in around him. He will never know.

SEPTEMBER

The turtle—silent in the autumn-morning mist. Gold lion paws are printed on his shell. On his head. His eyes are red. But gold is what you see. Gold leaf prints, lion's paws. His ancient snaky head is wet. His shell is wet. He's beautiful and big. He's old and bright and washed by rain. His saurian feet are spotted gold, and scratch the cool and mossy stones. Old man, I love you in this autumn mist! I stand there staring at that shell as though I'd found a mound of gold. It's that remarkable.

He draws his head inside. He's had enough.

THE ASH TREE HAS those curious lumps of olive-brown seed-flowers much loved by migrating birds. The leaves, turned olive-purple, olive-green, rose-olive, purple-yellow, are full of those mysterious birds. Birds chunky, yellow, and tawny, with stout beaks. (Not grosbeaks, though.) Small grey birds with yellow streaks in tail. Unidentifiable all. Some bird thing incognito. Let them have their mystery. (One flew against the pane and fell. The cat was on it in one long grey arc. By some miracle I made her drop it, picked it up and set it out of reach. It seemed to be dying, and for a long time my empty hand throbbed with that soft, feathery pulse. But in an hour it was up and flown—and still unknown.)

THE CREEK IS BORDERED with willow and jewelweed and wild pea. The bees work the wild-pea vines, but there are no flowers. The great juicy leaves of the water plantain are curling and descending; its mist of white flowers has turned to a ball of green seeds. The thrush goes on seeking in the green algaed waters; lovely clumps of fountain grass grow there, sand and pebble banks are still clear under the water, and the gold leaves fall. I wait and watch the water for the muskrat's coming. Observe each widening ripple for its source. Ripples from falling leaves. Ripples from diving frogs, ripples from water spiders and drowned butterflies. Ripples from wind. But no little hay wagon plying. No muskrats today.

The jewelweeds are in violent agitation. The whole plant swirls and shakes in a private wind. The dangling heads of its orange flowers dip and shudder. The green, ruby-throated hummingbird is there with its small, fierce wings and beak. Its wings are propeller wings. It hovers like a helicopter, darts and stabs, its green scales flash and its body coils like a fish. Its feeding is an assault, a frenzy. It can't cool down.

Enormous dragonflies haunt the muskrat pool. They are green and blue and of an evil and unusual size, as though born of this overfertilized water. Their heads are humped, their wings forever invisible.

They never seem to rest. Of the ten thousand varieties of dragonfly known—by someone—I can only guess this is a skimmer, for it flies low all the time. I would not want to see its water nymph if it is of such a size. They well may latch onto a swimming shrew, or naked human toe.

The sound of the water washes the day away. Carries the Sunday acid and sand out of the soul. Sunday's a bad day for me. Always has been. Hydrochloric acid in the stomach, from the moment of opening gummy eyes. A gritty dynamo starts inside. Panic, impatience, a sense of abysmal failure—well documented by the time day is done. But here, by this water, this sound of running water, a stillness descends. A water thrush comes, a dark thrush, almost black, with an aura of green. His breast is streaked, he is large in the late light.

He hops slowly from rock to rock, examining, snail hunting; his wet feet track the stones. He does not bob and jerk as much as usual. He is running down as the day ends. A black-and-white warbler marked with script flies down. Disappears. No warbler stays visible for long.

Down the wandering rocks that mark the stream's course goes the thrush. The bubbles mark the stream's course, too. I try to come to terms with these bubbles. They sparkle like true things of water. They descend small waterfalls, are sucked under, reappear, drift in silver groups, rush on when the current rushes. They are not too numerous today, they do not congregate in disgusting piles. Accept these silver things—these winking eyes of man. Lots and lots of man. He wants, she wants, to be very clean and to multiply. But I watch them as people of a conquered country watch the alien armies moving past them in the street. Their presence is a sign of irrevocable and spreading change. Nothing will ever be the same again. Nothing will ever be as good again.

This is a year of fruit. All through the woods red eyes of fruit. The wiccup tree has bright-red fruit, polished as red plums. The wahoo opens its curious three-partitioned lids, and the rich rose eyes dangle down. The orange eyes of bittersweet, the blue and clustered eyes of moonseed. Red eyes of turtles and red-eyed vireos. And the dark and drying eyes of the wild grapes puckered.

This is a year of fruit. A papaw year. The silver-green papaws are everywhere. Clusters of four and three, heavy, well-developed ones and twos. The leaves are turning transparent, paper-thin and pale yellow. They hang down in huge, pointed ovals. Oriental and beautiful. A papaw grove is not of this land. It is alien and tropical. Its seeds *rassimina,* divided equally down the middle, custard apple, *Asimina triloba.* The sweet melon smell of the fruit comes later.

I feel an empathy toward this fruit. Green until old. Ripe with black spots. Possible dermatitis given by handling the skin of. Offbeat. Off-fragrance. Ripened by frost. Slow, heavy, fat, and green. Beautiful, the leaves, in all seasons. Exquisitely carved the red-maroon flowers. Hard and unusual, these flowers. Beloved of Grant, these tropical northern fruits with their decaying scent. And equally divided down the middle, divided down the middle, divided down. Divided. Down.

One could write a poem to the papaw fruit: O *Asimina triloba— custard apple, sweet green melons!* . . . But it is hard to take small fat things seriously.

At six in the morning walked the north pasture. Listened to the squirrel-hunting guns. Kept my hate to myself. Felt the valley mist. Saw a buckeye big as a cantaloupe. It is dry. The grass is grey.

Dry days. Brown patches of dry earth. The moles, who made this mess of dry earth patches, seem to have gone away. Woods are full of dry snakeroot. Armies of depressing green harpies, old green bats. Air light and dry. Hunt for hard masculine words. Bone. Stone. Rock. Shock. Hunt. Lock. Avoid the strangling, tangling, entwining vine of verbiage, wordiage—garbiage. . . .

Prayed to God for that desire which will never come again. The desire to be a great writer at all costs. It will not come again. I am too old and the price is too high. I can't give up all the rest of myself—my crowded self. All the undisciplined, poorly organized pack of women and children who live inside me. Self-indulgent, easily tired, short of intra-span; longing to clean house, watch birds, read books, paint pictures, walk in the field, walk in the fields, eat in the fields . . . die in the fields. And some of them want to save the world, clean up the cities and rivers, tear down the Pentagon.

Prayed to see the deer. The long-rumored, once-seen deer of this inland island.

If I sit here long enough,
God will come.

A gold and well-shaped vision
Speaking
Gold, precise, words,
Memorable and majestic.

If not God,
Then His emissary,

The panther with the cold, gold eyes
Of the wild autumn and the winter to come.

If not the panther
Then the deer,
The leaping, long-hunted
Sole surviving
Deer of the violated virgin forests,
Stepping down to the brown sewer waters
Where the gold leaves fall.

If not the deer
Then a great bird,
The Lord-God bird,
The woodpecker with a flaming crest
And the bill that could make a cavity
Out of your chest if he willed to.

I'd settle for that.

No? Well, then
The autumn water will let loose a mink
Wet-furred, snake-headed,
Black coolness in the burning leaves.

If not a mink, a squirrel,
The lost red squirrels with fur like threads of gold and fire
Rippling the moss, the level logs.
Big eyes. Dark hands.

A chipmunk then?
They're quaint.
Striped, bulgy-cheeked. Flag tails.

Alright, a mouse.
If I sit here long enough
I'll see a meadow mouse.
They have big eyes, round furry bodies,
But no tails.

The leaves keep falling in the wind.
The shadows of the leaves leap up like fish.
And if I sit here long enough
The trees will all be bare.
Rocks covered with their golden scruff,
The big cold mouth of winter cough
And gum the whitening air.

So
Failing God, panther,
Bird and deer;
No mink, no squirrel,
Neither chipmunk nor mouse,
We'll settle for anything, I tell you!
And here it comes.
Singing its cheerful little autumn song,
Its winter song,
The only song it knows in fact.
Brother Cricket,

Small and armored,
Hearth and home and polished coffin,
Fiddler of the darkening nerves,

You're not what I'm settling for.

BUT ONE SHOULD MAKE no bargains with God. He holds the bag. "Bring me a deer, bring me this, bring me that . . . make me this, make me that . . . I'll believe."

Here's your deer. Now you believe. Now you're done for. I've got you. Get out of the woods I have made you love. Get away from the deer I have shown you. You believe in Me now. Get back to My work, which has no deer, no mink, no woods. Which has only people and suffering forever and ever and ever. . . .

THE POND ON THE hill has shrunken down to a ball of wet, wild, feathery algae—*Chara,* stonewort. Evil black mud lies under the waterline. Great porcelain thrush-spotted frogs grow sluggish under the willow roots, those red-net, water-seeking roots, delicate and fibrous, left when the water level drops. Good farming on the land across the road has done this to the pond. You plow the fallow land and save the storms. Big chocolate clods drink up the rain. No more run-off from the hard gullied alleyways of old neglect. The frogs go leaping over the algae like chunked skipping stones. Splop. Splop. They could go from shore to shore on the algae mass.

Down in the bottom, somewhere under the last four feet of dark water, is a great white leather saddle with a vicious mouth. A snapping turtle who came lumbering and lurching up the ravines from some drained pond or swamp miles away.

Old people who live too long come to resemble turtles. As though time turned in a curve, and down they go to the reptiles again. Not the little wet naked frog they were born. But the tortoise. Cold eyes, sagging circles of skin, the nose becomes beak. The shell of sleep.

Around the pond, half girdling the shoreline, run the cattail roots. Joining the great upright leaves, the cigar-brown tails, and sprouting the wet, white horns of coming shoots.

Examined root to flower, it is a miracle of wrapping. White sheath on sheath, twisted around and around, joining the rust-red jointed scorpions of root, covered with succulent hairs, wild-looking when dug up and thrown sprawling, with its black mud, white horns, brown hairs, on the dry white land.

The digger emerges like Neptune, a chilled, rake-bearing man, covered from the knees down with black oily mud that smells of coal. Algae hang like seaweed from his rake and from the algae pop grey tadpoles, greasy, with winking eyes.

What rises from this pond at night? The algae-dripping shapes with horns. Small eyes winking from their matted hair. I know. You know. This memory-matted circle of old rains. This footprint left when God's great mammoths shook these dinky hills. But now all's shrunk. We wait for snapping turtles. We're lucky to see a tadpole motor up, open its jaws and snap a drowning bee.

Lucky? We're lucky for more than that. There won't be many more days like this. No winter wind's bite. No summer's bite of bugs. Grab. Grab. Snatch the sulphur wings. The gold walnut leaves. The white butterflies in pairs. The wasps glitter. The dragonflies are red. Blue. Green. Black and blue. Green and blue. Turquoise, crimson, green and gold. One small pond, one big cold cup of water, swarms with life. Even the cat-tails have their own aphids—flat, tough, green, made for the reeds.

The shoreline is covered with dried tracks of children, raccoons, water birds. Aimless cuneiform messages, saying only, "I was here."

Think of the tracks made and vanished! The scents, the sounds, transformed, wiped out. Regard with awe and respect the waste of nature! The plan was prodigal.

The willow leaves are sweet in the warmth of the sun. They fall and drift and dry, curled like fish above the roots and mud. The broken wormwood is fragrant. A spice smell stronger than the mashed mint or the drying willows.

The redwing blackbirds are gone—to gather in late-planted cornfields. And so the carefully guarded nest among the rushes becomes the cause of torment. The sound of guns and explosives to drive them from the fields carries two miles down the valley and bangs against the windows and boxes the ears.

The birds are gone, but the pond is full of frogs still. Emerald lumps in the water. Iron frogs on land, with great gongs in their heads. The great hippo heads stare. A little light winks off and on under a chin. Off and on, off and on, out and in, the pulsing of its throat. The slow and guttural whoor-whoor comes from the reeds. There is the annoying twitter of invisible birds. The bushy breathing of the willows.

Doves descend to drink. What a travail is their landing, takeoff, and even flight! Their wings rip and fight the air. They land lurching and staggering. They waddle like geese on their tiny pink feet and sip the water. They are nervous. They see me. "The big blob is behind the willows." They wrestle themselves up into the air. The sound of ripping silk, and they are launched again. Only a minute grey feather is left. No marks of feet in the mud.

The bluegills come to the cracker crumbs. One is six inches long and rimmed with lavender. One crumb causes ripples six feet around. The crumb explodes. They drag this hookless bait under. The tadpoles rise and bite.

There is a hissing in the dry reeds. The insect *nnnnnnnn* goes on and on. Suddenly a wind smashes into the calm. The glossy surface is an avalanche of silver. The cattails bend and dip, wildly running both north and south. The delicate new blue dragonflies are blown off in a shower. Yellow leaves fall and are carried shoreward and shoaled.

Clouds cover the sun. My spirits slope and droop. The wind is cold without the sun. The saurian blood can't cope with change. Where is the old leather pancake with the spoon head on the long neck? Necklace of frog eyes. Foul hissing. Cold eyes. It's too early to sleep. Where *is* he?

THEY SAY A COLD front is coming. Autumn and winter. The king is being born. Snow has fallen out West already. The sky is getting grey. An ominous softness fills the air. Pond smells rise. Dry cattail odors, willow leaves and mud. It is getting darker and darker. A storm is coming.

The rain came. A deluge of water and yellow leaves. Now wet hay, wet weeds, wet leaves smell sweet in the sun. The bees come around. The cardinals dry out quickly. (There is hardly a more hideous sight in nature than a molting redbird in the rain.) A female scarlet tanager arrives. A yellow bird with a glowing breast. A thing that comes and goes so quickly, an almost subliminal vision. The female rose-breasted grosbeak. The mysterious Quaker-grey birds. One much larger than the other. Yellow underflushing color. There are two types of bird silhouettes—the kind you can draw with one line and the kind you add a tail to. That helps some, as the maddening migrations begin. Birds slinking through the well-covered, leafy trees. Colors winking off and on like Christmas-tree lights. Here it is. There it is not. Gone. Suddenly, the woods full of warblers. Every bird different. All with some variation of that basic warbler coloring, grey-green, green-yellow, yellow-grey, green-grey, black-striped, yellow-striped, and so forth.

WATER SMARTWEED LINES THE creek. There are two kinds, the reddish lady's-thumb, and the white. Something rushed up with a roar of wings from the pool beyond the weeds. Wild ducks, from the sound. The light comes through the maple leaves. A gold light, not a cathedral light, but the light shining down through the canvas of a tent, that seemingly sourceless diffusion and glow.

A great blacksnake, of serpent size, flowed loudly through the leaves. It lives near the rose-quartz stone, Old Scratch, the devil. The snake is good. I do not love it, but I hate those who kill it out of fear. There's a lot of lust in their killing. In the pasture we found the body of a snake with its neck broken. A rich brown snake—a harmless watersnake, but resembling a copperhead.

I know the scene as though I had been there—the shouts, the fear, the excitement, and the joy of killing. It was not killed by mistake for a copperhead, but because it was a *snake*. In the set minds of men and boys all snake is poisonous and must die. All around him were sticks stout as staves, broken and flung as though someone had scattered the faggots of a fire. A curious scene. The sticks more terrifying than the great dead snake.

The leaves begin to fall, and they float downstream. Each falling leaf makes wide ripples in the pool. The wings of dragonflies beat up the water without ever touching it.

The birds make a *churm* sound. Little things, with the color of rich egg yolk with black streaks. Phoebes and peewees, thrashers and chickadees. The great grey boneset lines the stream. Its leaves have silver fuzz. Its flowers are white and woolly. It makes a fine bold stand behind the rocks. It's a drug plant. Good. And has a beautiful poisonous cousin, the white snakeroot. Bad. From the view of man and domestic beast.

The vegetable world is full of poisons. Some, like the hydrocyanic acid of the bitter cassava, can be boiled away. Exposure to heat dissipates the poisonous principle. Manioc meal is made from it, healthy and nourishing.

But some cherish their poisonous principle for their own life's sake. Our walnut grove, our orderly grove of *Juglans nigra,* exudes the toxic juglane from its roots and has maintained the slender ranks of its own kind for thirty years.

Euphorbia inhibits flax, thistles discourage oats. *Artemisia absinthinum,* lovely fragrant weed, kills everything one meter around, by means of the absinthe in its fallen leaves. (Except for the deadly datura, which has a poison of its own.)

But the most ingenious life-by-poison principle lies in the shrub guayule (giva-yoola), *Parthenium argentatum* of northern Mexico and Texas. This large and bushy virgin thing insures its desert life by killing all around it, including its own kind. Little guayules leave home fast. Ask to be borne in favorable winds. Their monstrous mother gives them life and death. She needs that spot of sand and needs it bad. The Aztecs make footballs of the guayule.

IN THE LAST HOURS of September, sat beside Brian's pool under the sycamore roots. Listened to the monotonous *nock-nock* of the squirrels, the *wiccup-wiccup* of some bird. It was warm. A mosquito came. The pale, shy thrushes with egg-shaped breasts, lightly speckled. Great ferns held up the hillsides. A hickory with enormous roots seemed to hold up the rocks, hold up the hills, hold up this little world. The papaw leaves are yellow and transparent. Great paper paws.

This is the last water in the pure creek, and something will come to drink. You mark my word. And something comes. A chipmunk arrives. Takes a couple of sips. Goes.

A cool smell comes up out of the mud. I dig a mine in the wet gravel. The fly-bees' humming buzz is loud in the asters over my excavation, over the pool of wet leaves. A plant of self-heal has microscopic orchids, a green pine-cone head. What does one find in this teacup mine? A pale, sprouting seed without a name, a small ant, a small spine of a sea thing millions of years old, a fossil coral. Fossil shells. A little stone striped like a melon seed. If one dug on and on, what would one find? More of the same and more of the same. Little pale gritty things, biting things, ancient things, crystals and centipedes with a thousand legs. . . . Do you dig me, Jesus? More and more of the same.

I THINK OF GEORGE FOX's "infinite ocean of love" beside this last small pool.

OCTOBER

Cold. A cold, damp day. The snakeroot like it, they look very fresh. The glory of the red maples is upon us. The yellow of bitternut hickories. Willow yellow. Sunlight yellow. Drove a motley crew of dogs from the woods. A brown-and-white hound, a pregnant beagle, a bastard spaniel. It's cold in the wind, the air thinning before one's eyes. The redbirds are still a molting mess. They should feather up soon, or freeze. The sky is a heavy, cold grey. The wet leaves have a cold sound. A great woodchuck came crashing through the goldenrod. Never saw one so beautiful and big. His fur rich brown-and-black as sable fur, his tail of noble size. Except for his stupid bucket-shaped head, he might have been a sable.

There are flocks of sparrows now, soft brown with white-circled eyes, and sparrows with white mustaches. There are the tomtits, as always. So accustomed are we to the titmice, we must find something new about them. Have they idiosyncrasies? Exude poisons? They eat many bugs. Have five to eight eggs (chickadees five to thirteen). Suddenly the trees sprout warblers, soft, flying feathery olives, working the leaves for insects as fast and as furiously as shrews.

A cuckoo flew by, going south.

I live on an island of sanity: the island of this place. I am fortunate. I no longer ask why. The small animals, the birds go about their ancient and patterned ways. They do not enlarge their territories or change their patterns in order that they may kill and die more quickly. They do not care about us one way or the other. They do not know what we are doing. They do not know what we have done. I come before them, a five-foot five-inch shape, giving off what particles of warning smell I do not know, but I am not a shape of known guilt to them. I do not stand for anything that man has done to man. Of that they know nothing.

THE WIND IS FROM the south. The leaves falling in dry showers. Our autumn is not Keats's "season of mellow mists." Ours is brisk and dry. Nuts fall with gunshot sounds. It is beautiful, but it is not a dream. Silver gnats dance, but they look like go-go dancers to me, mechanical, trapped in an insane pattern. A shower of gold leaves falls in the sunlight. I think of Danaë's rain of gold. Jupiter was all those cold tickling coins on her stomach. . . . Soon all the trees will be bare. Is late autumn more honest than midsummer? It depends on what you want to see. What is the character of the nudist? It would be interesting to know. The skeleton of man is not the man. The naked man is the man. And yet one could question that. Is the shivering man the whole, real man? The thinking man is the whole man, and you can't think well when you're cold.

Is the naked and leafless tree any more the true tree than the whole tree with its leaves? Images betray us.

Mornings of hoarfrost in the blue valley. Each leaf of the forsythia rimmed in silver. Frost blue on the roof, on the grass. When the sun came up, the yellow maple leaves ran with melting ice. Frost-loosened leaves slipped down like rain. The air was pure and full of the smell of wet leaves. The spider webs had silver balls. The bluejays came. Sailing in, landing like big blue airplanes.

I saw a mole, a mole big as a saucepan, his grey silky fur spread out all over the ground, trying to get back down in his hole, out of the frosty morning. He squeaked and struggled. I could not see his head. It was as though something did not want him underground. I never saw any mole so big!

The quail are gathering. A flock of twenty got together after much calling, twittering, cooing. Only two seemed the young of this season. The lookout leader was puffed as an owl, turning his head above this edifice of feathers—right . . . left . . . to the woods . . . to the house. The yard seemed to swarm with quail. Then, suddenly frightened, instead of whirring off in a mass flight each quail zigzagged, pointed and crouched. All in different directions—a confusing pattern of shrewd design.

The maple gold is fading. Leaves of astonishing beauty lie in the grass. The quail go down to drink. A chickadee bugs them like a bee. Zooms in, zooms out.

The walnut spills huge squashy nuts big as melons, green and odorless. All size. No scent.

The phantom flicker came in full view at last. Have heard only his voice for weeks—that deceptive kingfisher whickering. He lighted in the grass for one full, glorious minute. His wild eyes, the stark black V on his neck, and the rainbow spots, all displayed. But he's a big, shy bird, and he left at once. He has no trust in the sword of his beak.

The male quail spread out the blue fans of their tails. Sidle like peacocks.

Now is the season of the autumn browns. The prickly buckeye bursts and splashes open. Bright shining nuts, like shining eyes of deer. Like polished jewels, they fall among the polished leaves. Bright brown, leaf brown, quail, woodchuck, chipmunk brown.

AS THE SUMMER, WHICH is the day of the insect world, draws down to night, there is a vast moving to and fro, nervous waves of flying and gathering, interruptions in the old furious pattern of eating and being eaten. The delicate daddy longlegs weave unsteadily in and out of the fallen leaves, they gather in ghostly herds, lay their eggs and die. The brown field ants gather the eggs of the corn-root aphids, bear them tenderly as bundled babies down into their tunnels and care for them all winter, to release them when born in the spring. The apple aphid—who has been self-sufficient and productive all summer, busily producing more females, winged and wingless, but females only, from her own body—feels the autumn cold, and suddenly produces wingless (and beakless) *males*. The males mate with the wingless females, and of this union comes *one* egg, carefully placed near a coming bud to wait for spring, and the aphid dies of old age at last. The cabbage butterflies of a late and untimely hatching flutter over the fields, where most of the flowers have died. The mice wander houseward, and the grasshoppers, grown enormous, with great glassy wings, having riddled the earth with eggs, hunt the southern sides of walls, and whir through the fields of drying corn. The jointworm sits in his dark cell in the stem of the wheat, the ground is tunneled with the hidden chrysalises of worms, and the bark covers small cocoons, and cocoons and chrysalises are hanging on twigs, in fallen leaves, and under the rocks. Eggs, pupae, adults, all in their infinite insect forms of house and shroud. And, as the days chill down slowly, the lady-beetles begin to feel a curious urge to gather together with their own kind. And, more mysteriously still, to find the same rock or log or cave, or even brush pile that sheltered their ancestors in the winters of other years. Their great-great-grandmothers have died sometime during the summer and cannot return, but there is probably some lingering and acrid odor in the winter places that guides the new autumn beetles back to their old home, for they come by the thousands, and sometimes, in the mountain rocks, by the millions.

There, in a dark, hidden hollow, under the arch of a snowbank or dome of frost-fringed leaves, they lie all jumbled together, like a hidden cache of bright jewels, their legs folded under as in death, and wait for the morning of spring again.

THE FLOWERS OF THE little terrace, the red and white flowers, have reached their last day. This was an odd sort of terrace they sat on. It was nothing but a big cistern top. The cistern is dug in the corner of a small plot of cleared land and all around it lie the woods, wild and leafy. The creek is full of great flat stones that would make a vast open platform. But each stone weighs a ton, so they stay right there. Instead, this six-sided ten-foot concrete cistern top with its round iron cover was our terrace. Our instant patio.

There was no room for chairs with the flowerpots, so the chairs sat around the edge, and you put your feet between the pots. When you watered the flowers the smell of wet concrete came up in the sun, and it smelled like childhood and the wet rim of the Jones swimming pool, and that pleasure, beyond all words, of being invited to somebody's pool in the summertime. A cool pool in the summertime. The "patio" was not a patio at all, being open to the sun but not enclosed, except by creeping grass. It had six giant pots of that red-clay color, the old-brick color, beautiful and plain, filled with instant flowers. Bought geraniums, bought petunias, bought salvia, and two pots of tomatoes. Behold, a garden.

We have never been much on gardening. The wild gardens of the woods have been enough. But in time one draws in, rounds up a little. Thinks, why not have flowers where one can see them? Is there more merit in the wandering pursuit of the elusive? Sometimes. But life is now. So here it is. Firm terrace, blooming garden, stamp-size, but here and now.

It was a pure delight all summer and all fall. Petunias big as moon-flowers, white, pure white, delicate and trumpet-shaped. And some double whites, like mounds of petticoats. They bloomed and sprawled. In their enthusiasm for life they nearly pulled their roots out of the pots. They poured down over the pot rim and lolled across the cistern top and spread out in the grass.

The salvia bloomed and shot out petals and rebloomed. It was a constant fire running up and down the spikes. It never stopped. Not even the pale waxy noose of the dodder could defeat it. The geraniums, the lovely spicy satisfying geraniums, those bushes of bright lily-pad leaves, were glittering bouquets of flowers that gave off an incandescent light.

The hummingbirds came. They whirred and stabbed among the salvia flowers. Their bright metallic bodies twisted like fish. The vibration of their wings beat the leaves into a whirlwind.

Whenever the flowers were watered, and every evening, the toads came out. One small pot had a small maple rooted in moss, a natural bonsai from the woods, and two little toads lived in its roots. When you watered, the moss would move, and two small grey bubbles would rise, four bead-bright eyes. In dry times they sat very quietly, wearing moss blankets humped over their shoulders. There were five of these little toads, no bigger than fat pennies, on the cistern top. They hopped so lightly, it was no more a plop than a raindrop makes. A big toad cooled himself in the tangle of petunia vines. His body was soft and shapeless as a beanbag. His stomach the color of doeskin, his warty back rust-and mud-color, not elephant grey.

How about this toad, of which you are so fond? Habits? Life span? Family life, stomach contents? After all these years of affection, what do you know about them? Does she lay her eggs in water? How big is the smallest toad when born? Do they eat bees?

In Sumatra people died of poison after a feast of toad. What kind fell from the bad sister's mouth when she lied, or just conversed? Great toads, beyond imagining, actually exist. One sees them in the *National Geographic*. The toad in art. In literature. The *Wind in the Willows* toad. The archetypal hero or buffoon.

Friend of the gardener. Victim of child fiends. Not sought after for the jeweled eyes. Soft as doeskin gloves. Neither bright nor stupid. A long life, as wild lives go, minding his own business, which, like that of all carnivores, is the taking of life, winged and jumping life, to sustain his own. His little hands are cold.

The harvest spiders, the daddy longlegs, haunted this minute terrace as they haunted everything else for miles around. They walked, they minced, they embraced, they fought. They came in different shapes, colors, and sizes. They were delicate and dreadful. They had that sweet nasty smell of spoiled fruit.

Dr. Leakey says man survived to dominate the animal world because he neither smelled nor tasted good. So with the harvest spiders: survival, if not dominance.

The toads delighted us all summer. Their little damp hands, their eyes and soft, vibrating throats. Their slow plops and swift tongues. It seemed too good to be true, too good to last. It was. At noon, one day in September, a beautiful yellow grass snake coiled in the shadow of a pot. Then it flowed away, a yellow stream in the grass.

No more little toads.

FROST IS PREDICTED TONIGHT. Gather in the flowers, the last green tomatoes. Restore this terrace to a cistern top again. Concrete, iron lid and giant iron ring. The season's over.

IN THAT EERIE PORTION of our woods where the trees are all sick and there is fungus of a dry sinister kind, Grant found a great paper-wasp's nest. It was built around the terminal branch of a thin wand of a tree, bowing it down in an arc. And at the end dangled this huge excrescence of grey paper. Smooth, beautifully executed by the wet mouths of the *Vespa maculata,* the white-faced hornets. A great cone of grey creamy whorls. The wasps were sluggish. One sat miserably in the hole, a chilled guard. This wasp can make nests the size of bushel baskets, housing fifteen thousand, but this was a half-bushel size, and big enough.

WET WEBS LIE OVER the lawn and the hill. The wet, dead mullein leaves have silver balls.

The mullein is a beautiful plant. Soft blotter colors, soft leaves like rabbit ears. It is called *Verbascum thapsus,* or, better, velvet plant, or, better, mullein, which has a warm, green, cloudy sound. The thrips' nests are found in its hairy ears in the fall. There are many thrips in the world—the very name means a breaking into small pieces (in which it is the mother name of all insects)—but the *thapsus* thrips have a woolly home and a peculiar mouth, well suited to destruction. The mullein, although beautiful, may give you dermatitis from those green *mol* ears.

"Out of this nettle, danger, we pluck this flower safety…" They say if you grasp the nettle firmly enough it does not sting. That's a lie.

It is terrible to wake at night and be unable to breathe. To feel one is dying. And when it passes, there is a weight left. The knowledge that all over the world human beings wake in prisons, wake in hospitals, wake in pain. Wake, and their pain does not pass.

This terrible year draws to an end. Young people are beaten and jailed because they will not kill.

> *The awful weight*
> *Of Christian hate*
> *Informs the fist*
> *In the eye of the atheist.*

Informs the club on the skulls of our sons who will not kill.

The world is dying of misplaced sentimentality. God hardened Pharaoh's heart. Now it is time to harden the heart of Moses.

A cold wind begins from the east. The wild fox drains out of me. The old hound pads toward the fire.

NOVEMBER

Is this rushing sound the stream, or the rain, or the robins? They are gathering in the ash trees black with rain, where the black seed clusters hang like wild grapes. Everything is wet and soggy, wet and warm, wet and chilly. The robins are the color of the wet oak leaves. Their breasts are quilted in triangles of feathers. Their eyes have white circles around them, and under their curved bills is this stern whisker pattern of feathers. They pluck up the leaves as though the leaves were worms. They have a listening stance. The robin is a large, refreshing bird. A sturdy bird. An oak tree of the bird world. He will be going soon, leaving the leaves disturbed and scratched in mounds throughout the woods.

A wet squirrel comes. Goes. An ugly little beast half mad with fleas. The quail are black with water. Clear raindrops hang on all the twigs. A delicate suspension on the young beech branches. There is nothing quite so beautiful as a clear, clean drop of water.

The robins are singing in the rain.

It is clearing. The cellar has pools of water. The wild grey cat is very lame. The pain must be bad, the way it limps. How will it live now? The sun through the soaked pines makes them glitter as though covered with ice. The red oak leaves are polished mahogany and scarlet in the sun.

Each day the valley opens farther. Stark, rain-black trees, white-washed sycamores, and that wet-paper orange of the last maple leaves. Now, in November, I do not see our lives as a whole. I see a great breaking up and out. A formless and violent eruption. Like magma, or great ice floes cracking and grinding as from some great internal disturbance, and pressure from the violent heart of earth itself. It is as though the very stability of the physical earth, founded on gravity, were changed. The magnetic poles seem shifting.

This force of formlessness means both disaster and freedom. Many of the young will be freed, many lost. Freedom is no guarantee of anything. It is only defined today by what it is not. What it *is* takes forms strange and of infinite variety—bizarre as in a masquerade.

For the true believer, great arms held the world together. For *this* believer, those iron arms have dropped away.

I look down into a beautiful valley. Our land—the kratogen—that portion of land remaining unchanged by earth movements in its vicinity. Woods full of second- and third-growth trees, maples and bass, wild cherry and ailanthus, ash and sycamore and oak. Great trees, but not as old as time. Look down, look back on fifty-seven years. Shudder. Look west through the leafless trees across the ridge to the Pacific Ocean where the once-children are. Children riding the breaking ice floes. Listening for the explosion and the lava. Can you ride the lava?

Can one write one's inmost heart to be read? I doubt it. Carol teaches me. She teaches me tolerance by her own kindness of heart and lack of corruption. By her newness in the world she renews my soul.

We grow by blows of various kinds. The sight of my rigidity in her big eyes is a blow. Suddenly I see the stark revelation: people's bodies are their own. Toes, nails, viscera, skin and hair—oh, hair—all that hair is their own, their own. Our judgment, our morality, is the morality of a pair of scissors. Since when did a pair of scissors stand in the pulpit, or be the ninth judge in court?

We need forgiveness. It is cold out here in the chapelless world. I'm no druid either. No hawk, no snake, no great tree is going to forgive me. Whatever there is of God is in me.

The war goes on. More terrible, fierce, more senseless with each day. Democracy is a weird thing these days. It all depends on whose ox is being gored. It all depends on how you read the numbers. And it all depends eventually on there being fewer numbers to read. No government can take care of each and all, but democracy becomes less and less capable to cope as the numbers increase. If we want to save law, we shall have to stop our lawless, fertile sprawl. We shall become—a disgusting image comes to mind and it is deadly accurate. We are in a great glass bowl, we fertilize, we multiply; like fish we spawn, like algae we divide, like frogs we fertilize. The bowl remains the same, and someone's sperm will be forever in our mouths and eyes.

A SILVER HOARFROST ON everything one morning. The trees were wave after wave of silver to the horizon, where they met a silver-blue sky. Every small oval leaf of the honeysuckle and forsythia was fringed with silver. The hackberry twigs, delicate as cobwebs. Leaves fell straight down. The sun began to melt the frost. The green leaves had an icy shine.

The frost and the sun and the melting on the forsythia leaves is a small pageant. The leaves are gold and green and purple, and all shades of brown and gold and green and purple. The melting frost glitters, the wet leaves glitter. The late gold flowers give back the light. A frosted spider line. The frosty jaja of the jays. Shadows of the pines are marked by blue frost on the grass.

First day of all the layers. Wool socks and scarf and boots again. But pleasant in the pasture, in the sun. Brown grasshopper made a loud noise coming through the leaves. The silver gnats danced up and down in the silver weeds. My head started bobbing up and down like a ball (the linking mystery of life, the invisible web that penetrates and binds. Rhythm. Very strange). The woods look distraught, the new-fallen oak leaves upside down and white. Spilled like paper over the brown leaves. Robins have been digging and scratching everywhere. The pool is brown, clear and quiet. One water spider left. The bubbles make one shadow shaped like a four-pointed star. This seems strange. Why should the shadow of a bunch of bubbles be one star?

Two bluebirds came to the north pasture. The red oak leaves still shine and cling. The ground is lumpy with black and green walnuts.

SPENT ALL DAY YESTERDAY dealing with great shoals of paper. The house much like the woods—a mass of fallen leaves, like the stream, a mass of white bubbles—waste, undone, unfinished, unanswered . . . the newspapers, the pamphlets, the magazines, the leaflets, the letters, the requests for funds, the bills. I shuffle about. Shuffle the papers. Stack and restack. Throw into the wastebasket. Burn the wastebasket. Rearrange. Seeking that order in a room which can never be found in life.

A smell of fish in the kitchen. All the boiling cinnamon and mace and lemon rind cannot erase it. It is hard to breathe, as though one were pushing up between living cells full of slag.

The wild cherry that leans over the house has taken a beating from the years. It is full of dead limbs, it is strangled by the hairy arms of the Virginia creeper. Its black crocodile-bark, like cracked clay, put here and there, has been riddled by locusts. Its leaves have been devoured every year by the tent worms. Its knot-holes are faces of wrinkled owls. Doves light on its dying branches. The next squirrel is going to bring the branches down. That dead, stumpy arm held an opossum one night. A fear-frozen young one sent up by dogs.

Nobody calls the opossum noble. Survival through silence is not considered a great virtue. Nevertheless, it is worth looking into. What have you to tell us, small abominable-smelling brother? (Lethal is the word for those odorous clouds they leave behind them in the summer nights.) Do you tell us not to "take arms against a sea of troubles"? "Arms against a sea of troubles"—that's the sentimentalist's motto—jabbing the ocean with a bloody spear. God, I loathe the sentimentality we are drowning in. We are killing with.

COLD AND SUNNY. NOTHING like the sun for making a dry, dead tree look dry and dead. These days children huddle miserably in the leeward side of schools. (This is a personal memory—most kids like cold, sunny days. They run around and shout, and punch each other.) I saw some battery-warmed socks in a catalog. Might send for them. These big windows surely let in the cold. I am in a hateful mood. One of the days in which one feels he has to invent his life all over again each morning.

When all the nests start looking like Christ's crown of thorns, when all the trees are crucified gorillas, that's just nature's way of telling us we're mad. There are few things uglier than a dead wild-lettuce stalk. It is tall, ragged, black-brown, and very ugly. An archetypal witch.

Here are the black trees. The grey trees. The brown trees.

There are the fallen leaves. The brown leaves.

Here are the grey birds, the black birds, the brown birds.

There is the grey sky, the grey hills. The brown weeds. The grey seeds. There is the brown water, the grey water. The green moss.

Where is the grey squirrel, the grey mole, the great grey mammoth?

A sparrow comes.

A sparrow's not just a sparrow. Is it English, field, or song? Is it Lincoln, chipping, white-throated? Is it fox, whiteheaded, or marsh? What does God write in that book when He sees one fall?

November, the eleventh month, is the ninth month of the old Roman calendar year.

The flowers of November: dandelion, forsythia, violets.

The birds: the usual crowd.

The colors: grey, brown and black.

The animals: in holes. Or hunted down.

The stars: I don't look at stars much. Too cold. Cricks the neck.

The rosettes: mullein and teasel. I boiled the teasel heads to soften them. They turned greenish, and the bristles pleasant as babies' brushes. Gave them black pin eyes. The children at the school like them. Probably had secret plans to prick unsuspecting friends. The acorns had inhabitants. Fat white grubs that came alive in the warm room.

"What's the smallest thing you know?" I asked the children. "What's like making a mountain out of a mole-hill? You've never seen a mountain or a mole."

"An ant."

"What's big?"

"A building."

"What else is small?"

"A termite's small."

"What's bigger than a termite?"

"A rat."

WILLIAM CULLEN BRYANT WAS born November 3, 1794. According to the introduction in the Household edition of his poems, a brown book with gold leaves on its cover, 1898, he was a "lad exceedingly frail with a head the immensity of which troubled his anxious father. How to reduce it to normal size was a puzzle which Dr. Bryant solved in a spring of clear cold water, which burst out of the ground in or near his homestead, and into which the child was immersed each morning, head and all, by two of Dr. Bryant's students, kicking lustily, we may be sure at this matutinal dose of hydropathy . . ."

> *When thoughts of the last bitter hour come like a blight*
> *Over the spirit . . .*
> *Go forth under the open sky . . .*

It's not the last bitter hour, but the present bitter hours, "stern agonies" of the living, not the "shroud and pall," that drive me forth under the open sky. Or a restlessness of the pooled blood, too long stagnant, filling with things that love a quiet marsh. But, O God, Great Oak, or whatever we cry to in our familiar agony—O for the great calm and faith that smoothed that mighty oversized brow of

Bryant, that pushed that great calm pen through a million words for eighty-four years, until, as we are told, "his capacious spirit passed out into the unknown. . . ." Capacious, there is a word for us! What would I not give for that spirit. Capacious. Oh, the warm, generous sound of it. Like a great wool cape against the wind. A shepherd's sheltering cape, and his arms full of lambs, his faithful collie at his knees.

And what's this net, this torn burr-plastered thing? My spirit, wet with weasel fur. . . .

LAST DAY OF NOVEMBER. Snow coming in from the north. Big squashy footprints full of grey water in the snow. Birds wild as though coming to their last meal. Fifteen quail with the same black, bull-headed leader. In birds a little difference goes a long way. The brown creeper creeping. Birds jousting for position everywhere. Woodpeckers pushing each other off the leeward side of trees. The grey air full of red, living flames from the cardinals.

A false alarm sent the quail exploding against the windows and walls. Then they regrouped under the forsythia cage. Two lost came running from the south with their seedy whimper, "Where are you, where are you?" The green grass spikes up through the snow.

The rain that came before the snow is freezing on the twigs. The vines have buds again, ice-folded flowers. The birds fly up and down like notes. Displace each other on the scale. The music would be odd. Both gay and irritable.

The rain and snow have stopped. The wind blows on. Drops freeze. It is a dark metal-blue day. In the heart of the honeysuckle it may be safe and warm. These green and shaggy vines that lumber along the fence, frosted with snow, balling up into great heads at the fence corners. Look like the pageant dragon that romps the street in Chinese festivals. Wrens disappear into its leafy mouth.

The fence rail where the whippoorwill plastered himself one April evening is a long line of wet snow. The fox-mange patch of hillside has a white scruff of snow.

The Old King is coming.
A rain of spears precedes him.
Long white knives.
Hounds and wolves enter the valley.

Gather the lambs together!
Hide in the hollows.

Good things are coming down the valley.
Who will hide them from the hawks?
Who will stand between them and the eagles of the King?

They are moving and the eyes have seen them,
Gold eyes of hawks,
Cold eyes of eagles.

Poor little band
Poor little travelers,
Poor little Good Things,
Singing in the snow.

The sky is changing. There is no more terrible color than that cold whiteness where the sky meets the horizon. That white metal rim that makes grey clouds seem soft and kind.

Now the whole sky is smooth and white. An enormous white page. Nothing written on it. No enormous message. Nowhere the words we should see written all over the world. *Stop the killing.*

All is white and cold up there. The heat is down here, in these smoldering fires of frustration, in the lives of black people, in the lives of the poor, in the lives of all who want the war to end. The land is red with it—under this cold white sky where nothing is written. This sky, this white eyeball of a white man.

DECEMBER

Hoarfrost is silver all over the trees, twigs, and grass. Silver-violet shadows. Silver-blue hills. A great woodpecker comes, the pileated giant. Flattens his body against the bark. He is the blackest thing in the woods. He has a flaming crest and a probing bill. But he is timid, he hugs the bark to him. I can see the black quilting of his feathers. Then suddenly he lifts his wings. The whiteness is startling. He takes flight like a great ship in sail. Magnificent!

On a tree, bright bitter green with moss and pale-green scabs of lichen from head to foot, a squirrel is cleaning himself in the sunlight. He turns his back. His arched tail is hinged in two parts. One part is round, a big furry circle, and concentric furry circles within, white, grey and brown, and in the center the tail's tip hangs down like another tail, white, brown and grey. He is scratching and biting, thriftily eating his fleas.

The margin of the hill is a moving and flickering line of birds, strung out restlessly through the frosty leaves. Juncos, sparrows, chickadees, wrens and titmice and woodpeckers. The leaves jump up and down from prying and flicking bills. The goldfinches are around, in winter feathers of such marvelous subtlety that the shades of brown and yellow and green flow in and out under the black and orange wing bars.

High up in the sun, a starling is singing. Singing? Holding forth, putting out sounds. His throat vibrates. His peacock colors of purple and green ripple. He has a frosting of flecks over the royal black, and his eyes are mean and stupid.

A DOVE IS ON the ground. In this winter light it is very brown. Snow is frozen on its long, thin tail. The dove ruffles the brown feathers of its back, opens them like a pine cone. It walks slowly on its raspberry feet. A delicate white rim circles its eyes. Pink patches are on its cheeks. When other birds fly over it, the dove flinches. I think it is wounded. It pecks the grain and then slowly walks away. It settles in the leaves at the edge of the wood, and faces the cold, early sun. Slowly the dove's head sinks in its feathers. They expand around it like the petals of a great brown rose. Only one eye, white-rimmed, anxious, is still visible. After awhile the dove is gone.

I LOOK FOR BLUEBIRDS. Might they not seem auspicious omens in this hour? An auspice is a bird seer. One who tells omens from the flight or feeding of birds. An omen usually favorable, or predicting good. (Is it not the function of such omens to fill with happy thoughts that time between the prophecy and the disaster?)

In finding the meaning of auspicious, I got hung up on *hate,* and from thence to *hathi,* meaning elephant, and *hathi, grey,* a color which is yellowish green, and *hat homage,* a Quaker phrase, and *Hathor,* a cowheaded goddess of love, mirth, and social joy. I like the simple definition of hater: One who hates.

Slipped out quietly to avoid the cat, Pussywillow. Walked quietly past the glazed pond with its frozen plume forms in the ice. Walked over the December dandelion. A large gold one. A defiant cold gold object in the cold green grass. Saw the goldfinches, now brown, in the bleached cattail sedges—very sedgy, very beat-up, beaten down. Approached the cottage, and there on the window ledge sat Pussywillow, an enormous silver-grey dandelion with cold green eyes. She had been surveying my arrival from the time I left the house. I, visible as I peered about to avoid her, visible as I walked softly on the gravel not to arouse her, visible as I crept by the willows of the pond.

From thence she followed—or preceded—me. A great mass of all this puffy silver fur—before—behind. Peering down holes, leaping over leaves, knowing what was there invisible, who had come, who had hidden, in what mood the wild thing that had walked before us. Telling me nothing.

Some honeysuckle was still rose and green and saddle-brown. Had bright black berries of surprising size and softness. Big clusters of unwinking eyes. The masses of honeysuckle vines that mat out and are moving down the once-pasture from the fence line do not have berries. They are a great bushy crawling thing without eyes. The goldenrod is being pushed downhill.

The cedars grow all through the goldenrod, whose galls are woody, polished knobs. I searched each cedar for a little owl. Saw-whet or screech. The cedars have increased in numbers, come in every size now, the new growth is a delicate blue-green, almost a smoke put out by the prickly flame. The old nest of the cardinals that housed the cowbird orphan was tipped over to one side. No owls. Came back through honeysuckle strongholds that hold up the pasture from below. When the vine tides meet we will have a Sargasso Sea of vines. (Will the center vines live forever, as the seaweed lives in the heart of the Sargasso Sea? Or will they embrace and strangle each other, as the higher forms of life find it best to do?)

The coralberry bush is leafless now, a delicate scaffolding of red berries. Odd that the birds don't seem to want them yet. The fallen walnuts look like iron or blackened copper. Soot-black. As black as any vegetable thing can be before it hardens into coal.

I found my screech owl in an evergreen near the house. Was led to it by a cloud of jays and chickadees, screeching and probing. There he sat, brown-and-white feathers flattened against the trunk, his ear tufts thinned high to make him as small as possible. His eyes half shut. The chickadees stitched in and out the needles, very close. The jays shouted. He did not move, and at last they went away and left him with his delicate ears ringing.

DECEMBER, THE WHITE BOLES of sycamores. The blue-and-white sky. The white-and-blue frost. The early snow, more a frost than a snow. A rime of silver. The sky is blue, the land seems shrunken since the leaves have fallen. My blood is still thin. Water is frozen. The creek still runs, will always run from its great sewer source.

TWO YEARS AGO I started the path through the walnut grove with a corn knife. That path was made in an agony of spirit, a coming to terms with the concept of oneself as murderer. The stark taking to heart of this knowledge, as one would take a wild animal with poisonous teeth or fangs, and holding it there, this knowledge that as long as you pay the bills for this war, you are a part of it and whatever it results in. You cannot say (as we could say of Hiroshima), I did not know. *I know.* You know. It is known.

What, then, is the result of this embrace? Knowledge and knower become one. In the ensuing darkness that follows this question, dim forms move about. There is comfort in the vast company in which we find ourselves. We are all murderers here. You, I, my neighbor, and all the law's trustees. An unwilling, restless throng. But a warm throng. We are all engaged in keeping warm, keeping the lights low, keeping the soul's terminal sickness a secret.

Who is outside this huddle? The hope of the world is outside. The sons who will not go to war. The young who throw themselves in front of the war machine. The men and women who do not pay war taxes. They are outside the warm huddle and some are inside the walls of prisons. But they are free. They are the only free people in this nation.

ON THIS PLANET PAIN, the season of Christmas is upon us. The men of the communications media are gathering on the parapets with paper bags full of sugar water and mother's molasses. Their pens and voices are beginning to choke up as they see "time-honored traditions" being trotted out, wiped off, set up.

Orphan children are given a buying spree for Christ's birthday. The children leave the buses, their little faces radiant and eager. They are greeted by the genial owners of the store with fistfuls of five-dollar bills. Each child, the commentator tells us, may buy whatever he wishes. Some children can't decide. "But here's a little fellow who knows just what he wants. . . ." The voice is filled with patronizing, fatherly indulgence, and the camera focuses on a small child of eight, his innocent round face smiling, his arms filled by a toy machine gun as large as he is.

The manger scene is being set up in the park. I think it is a fine idea to recall this certain child on his natal day. Of all who come to stroll, or stand and stare at this plastic replica of God's son, some will be weighed down by monstrous ironies they feel, but cannot understand or really bear. To find this child, we are told, and to wipe out his dangerous power to come, Herod ordered the slaughter of young children throughout his kingdom. The child was not found, and he lived. Today the slaughter goes on in this child's name.

We think of children in this Christmas season. There should be services in all the churches for the children. For the children blinded and homeless in Vietnam, for the children robbed of childhood and turned into thieves and prostitutes, orphaned and mutilated. For the children who have been burned to death. There should be services in the churches for the children of the poor here at home, who have been robbed of their education, robbed of their heritage, to pay for this vast, mindless sinning. Childhood and manhood wiped out by war.

We think of the thousands of young men dead in the war as of this hour. The young men wounded, burned, blinded, paralyzed in the strange perversion of this child's teaching.

The Pentagon is the greatest power on earth today. We cannot absorb the Pentagon into an image. We cannot fit it anywhere in the natural world, relate it, compare it. There it sits, a terrible mass of concrete, on our minds, on our hearts, squat on top of our lives. Its power penetrates into every single life. It is in the very air we breathe. The water we drink. Because of its insatiable demands we are drained and we are polluted.

Nothing in the world is like this concrete monster. It is not a mountain. It is not a storm, it is not a hurricane, a pack of wolves, a flood. It is like the great god Moloch into which the children were thrown as sacrifice. It is the greatest unnatural disaster of the world.

We can call it a cancer in the body of the world—this five-sided concrete sore, full of neatly dressed and tidy human beings, who work to spread its malignant cells throughout the life of the world. Who work to substitute death for life. And make no mistake about this. No matter what is said is happening, this is what is happening—death instead of life. Death of the heart, death of the mind, and death of the body. We cannot even probe the final mystery of the cancer cell in the human flesh because of this great Thing's demand.

I SET OUT TO circle and crisscross the land in this last month of the year. Visit the three great stones. The oak. The mink crossing. Find the hornet's nest again. The quiet valley. Cross the ruined creek, the pure creek. Climb the snail hill, the north pasture, come home through the walnut grove and the woodchuck's small ravine.

That barren stretch of land, where the hornet's nest was found, I like the least of all the acres. This piece of land is strange. A graveyard of the woods. Here is where, if ever, the murdered traveler will be found. On this desolate dying patch of witch-rent.

There are thorns here, great clusters, grey and brittle, bouquets of swords. The underbrush is made of high weeds and raspberry hoops. Fallen trees and fallen limbs of trees litter the hill. Young trees are bent over by old trees, and all are diseased, covered with an unpleasant moss. A moss not truly green, but a whitishness. There is a purplish film over the one pine tree in all that mess of broken limbs. The Virginia creeper strangles the living and the dead. Its hairy roots spray out, dig in the bark. Some plants bleach to white, some blacken in death. This is a fit place for a rape, a murder, or the culmination of despair. Do the old trees come here to die? Why is this piece of land so cursed?

I could not find the hornet's nest. Each tangle of dead vines and branches; rotting logs and decaying snakeroot, looked alike. And then suddenly it was there, right in front of me. But an awful change had come over it. The great nest, like grey whipped cream, smooth whorls of paper cleverly designed, was torn and shredded. A dreadful pagoda, a thatched thing hung there, with its whole bottom torn away, exposing the open cells. Shreds and clumps of torn grey paper were scattered in the weeds. Was it birds? Squirrels? The branch it hung by was too delicate to hold anything heavier. Birds, I would say. Hanging on it and shredding away to eat the delicious white things within.

Everything seemed gnawed in these woods, rotten wood pulp exposed. Dead leaves of beeches rattling. Paths of hunters following the flat land above. Some harmony of hate here. I shall not come back unless I am still searching for some elusive darkness, some concentration of that vague enveloping misery which is my mortal cloak (shirt, skirt, socks, shoes, sweater and cap). Not even to watch this strange ecology develop. Here the witches come to die. Or to gather thorns for their winter weddings. They love it here. It has that fungoid nourishment they need. But not in the summer. In the summer, it is dry and dusty.

ONCE OVER THE RIDGE, a change begins. A profound change. Is it shadows in summer, or the way the water runs? The trees stop dying in confusion. They lie down and rest silently. The pure creek runs with rain. The moss is greener than Ireland. The rocks are green and clean. Great oaks are here. Whole and healthy. The shedding and scaling that went on before, like a tide of disease and dandruff, is all gone. The very fallen leaves are different.

It is a ravine, and very quiet except for the sound of the water. No birds. No chipmunks. Nothing moves but the water; nothing speaks but the water. It is clean water. The leaves are wet and deep and soft underfoot. That great tree leaning from one side of the creek to the other is a mossy bridge, thick green moss from root to crown where it was rimmed with snow last January. Bright green moss covers the roots of the bitternut tree that hold the bank both north and south and plunge straight down like thick legs of elephants into the small stream. Spectacular and almost grotesque, the velvet green of these roots. They are so powerful they disturb and satisfy. A rock holds a fossil shell, blue and silver, delicately veined.

I sit and rearrange the days, the words, the acts of all last week. Placing things as they should have been. Saying the things I should have said. Undoing that which should not ever have been done. But it's no good. It is only pain.

It is better to push on down the stream course with the banks dripping with sword ferns. This is winter. This is December. And here are all those green ferns in the warm grey sunlight! And tree trunks sprouting a fox fire of orange fungus, fat fleshy knobs like ears of corn.

The dead thicket of wild plum is green with lichen. Moss is bright green over all the stones. Michaelmas winter. Weather warm enough for the slime mold to be on the move. Humping and inching its film along the floor of the woods, flowing over and under the bark of fallen trees. Grey-violet shadows move along the ridge. Large unsubstantial clouds dissolve into a spring-blue sky, the sun moves downward to the grey grass, where the ground is littered with the big pocky balls of mock orange. Lavish in size, smelling faintly of bitter fruit. A yellow-green that shines like the sun. Nothing eats them that I know of, and they lie there all exposed and tempting. A wild mock. The trunks of Osage oranges are always twisted, the bark shredded; they are bent and tortured as though they fought from the hour of seed. They are very tough.

The doves are flocking. Easily frightened, ripping in and out of the fir trees as one passes, wheeling and tearing the air with their wild wings. Pinheads.

NOW, TIRED FROM WALKING, befuddled by something that seems to come from the leaves—an emanation—eyes hurting, I hunt a tree, a spot to lean against and sit down. Approach the rose-crystal granite rock cautiously. Observe its wet shining loveliness, keep my eyes on the log where the great blacksnake lives. A few steps forward and there is Old Scratch himself—long, moist, and coiled, savoring the warmth of this late spring, this intermittent sunlight. What an event! He does not move. I pass and sit on the ground against the tree.

Two old reptiles, we doze in silence. Nothing moves. Nothing calls.

The sunlight falls like a gold sweater on the shoulders. It dries the chilly mud. It is reflected in the bright pin eyes of the chickadee. It is a free and mindless benediction over the winter world. The dry pods of vines move with a small music in the breeze, not a wintry rattle.

What interval is this? What curious hollow that is happiness? The heart is a warm and humming hollow. I live. I am. This is not holy, this is not heaven. This is the ancient pagan hollow of the hand that holds the sun.

After awhile I get up and go through the warm brown spongy twilight. The creek is a rushing of tan clay. Old Scratch still lies there coiled. What will he do if he cools to torpor before he knows it and cannot make it back to his hole on time? In the west, a curious tower of clouds rises like a smoke signal, a brassy gold. And behind it, the blue sky opens before the night comes down.

ONCE IN THE YEAR there comes *the snow.*

There are all manner of snows, both cruel and kind. There is the snow that falls like needles and drifts in hard ridges on the dead corn-fields, is bitterly cold, coming down from the northwest and driving into the earth like knives. And there is the snow that people think of as *snow,* that actually comes very seldom, but is the symbol of all snows, the childhood miracle that remains forever an image larger than all the dreary, bitter or halfhearted snows that come before and after.

The snow falls slowly in soft, descending clusters like fairy snow-balls. It falls slowly, almost thoughtfully, and far apart. So slow, so far apart that children can stand and choose which cluster they want to catch on their tongues. The snow clings where it falls, lovingly and coldly to the barren twigs, pure as wool blankets over the dead grass. The wild-raspberry wires become tunnels of silver whiteness, the browning pine trees become white trees, and the grapevines are a still, white fountain of flowers.

Everything is still, so unbelievably still. We brush away snow from sheltered spots and spread out crumbs, and the chickadees, whose seedy voices are muffled in the snow, come, and the redbirds and winter wrens and quail. The thistles become flowers. The wild carrot blooms again.

The snow falls to the proper depth, to the exact moment when all ugliness is covered, to the weight that the twig and branch can bear and be beautiful without breaking. It knows precisely when to stop, when the moment of absolute perfection has been attained, and there it stops.

All night the snow remains motionless, unless a twig is shaken by an owl or a weasel. It hardens a little with a light, pure crust, to bear the weight of the wild things walking in the night, and to preserve itself for the daylight.

The morning comes slowly through the arches of whiteness in the woods, and comes more silently. It begins with a grey whiteness, and the sun is late. The ground is stitched with tiny tracks that end suddenly in round, damp holes, or stop and vanish as a small thing flew upward. The oval tracks of rabbits wander purposefully along the raspberry thickets, and the sycamore balls have little caps of fur.

It is best in this white greyness before the sun has come through the ascending clouds. The brooding, silent, closed-in world of snow and whiteness, motionless except for the birds, the grey juncos and the wrens, a timeless moment like an enormous pearl, a moment of stillness before the sun, and the thousand-diamond glitter and the rainbowed sound of light.

Even children, whose first thought is to tramp it with their big galoshes and scrape it into balls, stand for a moment in awe at their windows, on their porches, and drink in the miracle that is to become forever *snow* for the rest of their lives. The snow that is almost too beautiful to be borne.

IN THE YEAR'S END, without faith, without expecting an answer, we find ourselves crying, "Almighty and most merciful God, Maker of heaven and earth—Maker of earth—Maker of this beautiful and awesome world, stop this terrible and disgusting march of Thy people to destruction. Stop the killing!"

And God answers, "Mighty and unmerciful man, stop your own killing."

Which leaves us here in this white cold winter, in this orderly world of nature with its fine and intricate chains of life which man has broken, screwed up, and is preparing to strangle himself with, to find an answer. An imperfect answer.

We are dying of preconceptions, outworn rules, decaying flags, venomous religions, and sentimentalities. We need a new world. We've wrenched up all the old roots. The old men have no roots. They don't know it. They just go on talking and flailing away and falling down on the young with their tons of dead weight and their power. For the power is still there, in their life-in-death. But the roots are dead, and the land is poisoned for miles around them.

How can I hold such bitterness in this white snow on this lovely darkening land? Because there is nothing in all of nature that can compare to this enormous dying of the nation's soul.

IN THE LAST DAY of the old year a snow came down, a thin, grey snow. Very cold. In the late afternoon, this falling snow came down straight as rain. Fell straight like white rain down one's collar to the shuddering spine. Down on the crumbling cottage. Down on the dog tracks, down on the thistle leaves and over the wild green mint. It fell down like a blank white curtain, a final curtain over the last day of the year. Rung down, blotted out. And the coldness of night poured in from the dark ravines. It went down to zero in the night. And the new year began with awesome clarity.

ABOUT THE AUTHOR

Josephine W. Johnson (1910–1990) was a novelist and nature writer who in 1935 became the youngest person to win the Pulitzer Prize for Fiction for her first novel, *Now in November*. She began her studies at Washington University and went on to write eleven books over the course of her life. When it was originally published in 1969, *The Inland Island* became a beloved and critically acclaimed bestseller.